# EDINBURGH IN OLDEN TIMES

*Edinburgh Castle in 1670*

# Edinburgh

## In Olden Times

**DUNCAN FRASER**

STANDARD PRESS MONTROSE
MCMLXXVI

*By the same author:*

HIGHLAND PERTHSHIRE
GLEN OF THE ROWAN TREES
THE SMUGGLERS
EAST COAST OIL TOWN

© DUNCAN FRASER

Printed at the Standard Press
Montrose, Scotland

THE FRONTISPIECE and the illustrations on pp. 108, 119, 120 and 151 are from Wenceslas Hollar's engraving "The Citie of Edenburgh", in the Royal Library at Windsor Castle. They are reproduced by gracious permission of Her Majesty the Queen. The altar panel from the Church of the Holy Trinity (p. 35) is also reproduced by gracious permission of Her Majesty the Queen.

I am indebted to Lord Egremont for permission to reproduce four details from "The Siege of Leith 1560" — pp. 24, 73, 74 and 77.

The illustrations on pp. 67 and 68 are details from the 1544 map of Edinburgh in the British Library (Cotton MS Augustus I ii. 56) and are reproduced by permission of the British Library Board.

The two pages from Queen Margaret's "Four Gospels" (pp. 14-5) are reproduced by permission of the Secretary of the Bodleian Library, Oxford.

I wish to thank the staff of the National Library of Scotland for all their helpfulness in providing illustrations. Those on pp. 17, 20, 21, 29, 32, 37, 39, 40, 54-5, 62, 66, 99, 103-7, 109, 114, 130-1, 132, 134-41 and 144-5 are all reproduced by permission of the Secretary of the Library.

The jacket design and many of the typographical ideas, including the ornaments based on Gordon of Rothiemay's map, are by Mr Lawrie Harris, Brechin. The blocks are by Hislop & Day Ltd., Edinburgh.

The photographs on pp. 36, 38, 63, 86, 92, 96 and 112 are by Mr F. D. Cuninghame. Those on pp. 11, 18, 19, 45, 46, 48, 51, 58, 64, 65, 69, 78, 79, 80, 83, 88, 89, 101, 123, 125, 126, 129, 143 and 146 are by the author.

A*

# Contents

# Illustrations

# I

## In the Beginning

*Edinburgh from the Castle*
(For four centuries the North Loch was a prominent feature of this view)

EDINBURGH, you might say, was born untold millions of years ago, in a fiery inferno amid the rumble of earthquakes and the acrid fumes of burning lava. It was then that the rock on which the old town stands came bubbling out of the ground. And some twelve thousand years ago, when the land was perpetually buried in ice and freezing cold, a glacier carved this volcanic plug into its present shape, like a meteor streaking westwards.

The rock remained a landmark which could not be ignored. The Romans knew it well. It commanded one of their main trade routes to the north. And after they had gone, the Angles knew it even better, for they built a Dark-Age fort on its summit.

As early as the sixth century you find it mentioned in Aneurin's Welsh poem, the "Goddodin", when its name was Dineidin. But at that time, and for

centuries later, there was not even a straggle of houses up the castle rock. It was only when danger threatened that folk gathered their livestock and headed for the safety it offered. Though there were other hill-forts in the district, Dineidin by its very position was the most important of them all.

For many centuries it was wrongly thought to have got its name because this was the Burgh of Edwin, the greatest of the warrior kings of Northumbria. And, though it acquired its name too early for that, the fact remains that Edwin must have known it well. His kingdom extended from the Humber across to the west coast, and some say it included even the islands of Anglesey and Man. The Firth of Forth was its northern limit and the rock of Dineidin was an obvious strongpoint, a defence against the warlike Picts who lived beyond the estuary. Northumbria was not only the most powerful kingdom in Britain but a great cultural centre too, when Edwin died in 633 A.D.

For almost four hundred years after his death, the fort on its volcanic rock remained a Northumbrian strongpoint astride the coastal route to the north. But before the end of the tenth century the military might of Northumbria crumbled and the Scots seized this hill-fort. In 1018 they overran the rest of the Lothians.

It was not the Northumbrians, however, or even the Scots, who first brought Edinburgh out of the mists of antiquity. The credit for that goes to a Saxon princess who came from the south of England to be Queen of Scotland. Her brother, Edgar Atheling, lost his throne when the Normans invaded England in 1066. Four years later, with his two sisters, the Princesses Christian and Margaret, he boarded a ship for France and ran straight into the teeth of a raging gale.

The storm swept his vessel far off course, northward along the coast of England and Scotland, until it reached the Firth of Forth. There Edgar landed at North Queensferry with his two sisters and sought the protection of King Malcolm Canmore in his castle at Dunfermline. Soon after, Princess Margaret became Queen of Scotland.

There were many older people in those days who could remember when all the Lothians, as far north as the Forth, was still part of Northumbria. When Malcolm's father began his reign, only the rock of Dineidin was in Scottish hands. Yet in the few decades that had passed since then, the Lothians had become so much a part of Scotland that Malcolm Canmore was able to build a lodge on top of the castle rock at Edinburgh and use it for hunting expeditions in the surrounding countryside. It became one of his favourite haunts, for the great Forest of Drumselch, stretching southward from the foot of the crag, contained an abundance of "hertis, hindis, toddis and siclike maner of beastis".

Often Queen Margaret accompanied the King on those journeys across the Forth but her taste was more towards meditation. The King built her a chapel at the hunting lodge and whenever she came her two most treasured possessions came with her.

One of these was a crucifix which later gained fame as the Black Rood of Scotland. Even in her own time, her confessor Turgot tells us, it was of priceless value. Not content with the usual figure of Christ on the cross, her crucifix had his body covered with gold and silver and studded with precious stones. Another writer, Aeldred, tells us that its name was derived from the large black box in which it was kept. When you opened the box you found a magnificent cross inside — about three feet long and of pure gold studded with diamonds. The cross itself could be opened too, to reveal a fragment of the True Cross bearing a figure of Christ "sculptured out of massive ivory and marvellously adorned with gold". But there is some doubt about Aeldred's story, especially about the black box. The Black Rood is much

more likely to have got its name because the crucifix itself was black.

Queen Margaret had it with her in 1093, when King Malcolm left her in the hunting lodge, while he set off with his eldest son on a raid across the Border. For several months she had been unwell and within a few days she was gravely ill. By 15th November she was so weak that she had to be carried into the chapel for mass. Next day her stepson Edgar arrived from the south to find her at death's door. The Black Rood was in her hands and choristers were chanting psalms at her bedside. He broke the news she had been dreading — that the King was dead. A few minutes later the Queen died too.

By that time the enemy was approaching and her young children were in imminent danger of capture. So began the first of the rock's many tales of high adventure. With a November mist swirling around, Turgot took the children to a postern gate on the steep western side and they were led down a precarious path to the foot of the cliff, while he followed with the body of his Queen. When the enemy arrived, the hunting lodge was deserted. The mourners were already crossing the ferry for the Queen's burial in Dunfermline.

Her grave became a place of pilgrimage, where the sick went to be healed. But it was not there that the strangest of her miracles happened. The most incredible of them all brings us to her other most treasured possession, a manuscript of the Four Gospels. Like the Black Rood, it too was a work of art, illuminated in gold and other colours and ornamented with figures of the four Evangelists. Even the outer case was embellished with gold and jewels. Bishop Turgot tells us that one day a priest lost it while on a journey. Every inch of the long road was searched without result. And then, when all hope was fading, the book was at last rediscovered lying open and saturated with water, on the bed of a deep river that the priest had crossed.

A courtier dived in and recovered it. To everyone's amazement the leaves were still white, the illuminations unsmudged and the lettering as brilliant as ever. Before it was lost, the illuminations had been protected by fragile silk coverings. One of these was swept away by the current. But there was nothing to indicate that the book had ever been immersed for hours in water.

Nine centuries have passed since Bishop Turgot wrote that story of the book's misadventures and no one would believe it today without much more tangible proof than his word alone. That came in 1887.

At a sale that year the Bodleian Library bought a fourteenth century manuscript of the same Four Gospels, a little octavo volume with a shabby brown binding. For at least a century it had been in a Suffolk parish library.

Soon after it reached the Bodleian Library, it was found to be three centuries older than anyone had imagined. The handwriting and illuminations were typical not of the fourteenth but of the eleventh century. One of the illuminations too had lost its silk covering, and the vellum end-papers at front and back were slightly crinkled as if by water. But most remarkable of all was the fact that about 1100 A.D. someone had written a Latin poem about the adventures of this volume and pasted it on the flyleaf. Though the wording was quite different from Bishop Turgot's, in every essential detail the story was the same. The poem ended: "Eternal salvation to the King and his saintly Queen whose manuscript was so lately saved from the waves. All glory to God who saved the book."

Beyond any shadow of doubt, the Queen's own manuscript of the Four Gospels had been found again, after being lost for seven centuries.

\*     \*     \*

The oldest building in Edinburgh today is St Margaret's Chapel on top of the castle rock. Even its shape is unusual. for its walls are square on the outside and semi-circular inside. A chevron-and-lozenge design on the chancel arch is

*Treasure of a saintly Queen —*

uider̄ oculi mei salutare tuū · quod
parasti ante faciem omniū populorū ·
Lumen ad reuelationem gentiū · &
gloriam plebis tuae israhel ·

SECUNDUM LUCAM ·

IN illo tempr̄ · Intrauit ihc̄ in quoddā
castellū · & mulier quaedam nomine
martha · excoepit illum in domū suam ·
Et huic erat soror nomine maria · quae
etiam sedens secus pedes dn̄i · audiebat
uerbum illius · Martha autē · satage
bat circa frequens ministerium · Quae
stetit · & ait · Dn̄e · non est tibi curae
quod soror mea reliquit me solam mi
nistrare? · Dic ergo illi · ut me adiuuet ·
Et respondens · dixit illi dn̄s · Martha ·
martha · sollicita es · & turbaris erga plu
rima · Porro · unū est necessariū · Maria
optimam partem elegit · quae non au
feretur ab ea ·

PASSIO DN̄I NR̄I IHŪ XP̄I
SECUNDUM LUCAM :·

IN illo TEMPr̄ · Adpropinquabat autē
dies festus azymorū · qui dicitur pascha ·
Et quaerebant principes sacerdotum
& scribae quomodo ihm̄ interficerent ·
timebant uero plebem · Intrauit
autē satanas in iudam qui cognomina
batur scarioth · unū de duodecim · Et abiit
& locutus est cū principib: sacerdotū

*— Queen Margaret's 1000-year-old Four Gospels*

evidence of its age. There is similar carving at Leuchars, in a lovely little church that was built by a Norman nobleman, Saier de Quinci. At Dunfermline Abbey too there is the same kind of carving on the great west door. And you can see it again at Dalmeny, in a Norman church which is one of Scotland's oldest and most delightful architectural gems. In Edinburgh, St Margaret's Chapel is the only good example of genuine Norman work.

The very fact that you can see the chevron-and-lozenge design is proof, however, that this is not the chapel which Malcolm Canmore built. Queen Margaret was already dead when decorations of this kind were first introduced in Durham Cathedral. Her son, King David I, built the Norman abbey at Dunfermline and there is little doubt that he too built this chapel, in memory of his saintly mother.

It was due in large part to King David's inspiration that all through the next two centuries the whole country was involved in an urge to create new churches and cathedrals, priories and abbeys, with a craftsman's care, regardless of time and expense. Edinburgh itself, though little more than a village, must have been bulging with highly skilled workers. On top of the rock St Margaret's Chapel was only newly finished. Halfway down, the Kirk of St Giles was taking shape with its massive pillars and its grandly styled entrance porch. At the foot of the hill, work was about to begin on Holyrood Abbey, the most splendid of the three.

Though the abbey did not reach its final size for a century and a half, in its romantic origin it got off to a flying start. Ancient legend tells us that four years after David I became King of Scotland he decided to go hunting, one September day in 1128, in the woods around Edinburgh. His confessor tried hard to dissuade him, for it was the Feast of the Exultation of the Holy Cross and no day for ungodly pursuits. But the barons were not very devout and for once the King listened to them.

With hounds baying and bugles echoing, the hunting party swept down the slope from the castle into the woodlands of what is now the Canongate, and all the beasts came fleeing out in terror from their dens. One by one the barons chose their quarry and rode off in pursuit, until only the King was left. Then suddenly a stag, far more huge than any he had ever seen before, came charging at him.

The thunder of its hoof-beats and the span of its antlers so terrified the King's horse that it "ran perforce ouir myre and mossis away with the kyng", and all his efforts could not curb it. But the stag came pounding along still faster in hot pursuit. Hurling the horse and rider to the ground, it swung its great antlers at the defenceless King. He threw up his hands in a despairing gesture to shield his head and in an instant a miracle happened. There was no gashing blow. Instead, something slipped into his hands. And the stag, wheeling round, sped off like the wind to vanish in a moment before his eyes. Looking down, he found he was clutching a fragment of the True Cross. That night, in a dream, he was told by God to build an abbey at the place where his life had been saved. He sent to France for twenty experts as supervisors, and the work soon began.

Oddly enough, King David was not the only one who was attacked by an irate stag and saved by a fragment of the Holy Rood. So was St Hubert, four centuries earlier in France. And long before that St Eustace had exactly the same experience in the second century A.D. If you look at the burgh seal of the Canongate you will find a reminder of the Midlothian miracle, for the stag with the cross between its antlers is featured there. But that was an afterthought. It was only in 1453, in the reign of James II, that this began to appear on the abbey seal.

There is said to have been another miracle during the building of the abbey. When the choir was almost finished, a joiner fell to his death from the lofty roof. That night his body lay covered

by a shroud, in front of the high altar, and it was still there when King David arrived next morning. Telling the monks to sing the Mass of the Holy Ghost, he knelt in prayer beside the corpse. Then he uncovered the man's face and the dead workman was alive again.

King David, by that time, had two holy relics — his mother's Black Rood and the fragment of the Cross which he had acquired in his strange encounter with the giant stag. Keeping the Black Rood in his own possession, he died at Carlisle in 1153 with it clutched in his hands. His other relic, the Holy Rood, he had given to the abbey and from this it derived its name.

It is not easy now to realise the feelings inspired by relics like these. People had more unquestioning faith in those days and few ever doubted that the Holy Rood had come from the cross on which Christ was crucified. It had a long list of marvellous cures to its credit. And that was natural enough, for many lesser relics in churches elsewhere produced miracles too. A shrivelled arm-bone from the corpse of St Fillan was one of these. Its miracles began while the saint was still alive. In the long winter nights it used to glow like a torch when he held it above his head, and he read his books by the light of it. He kept its miraculous powers a secret until one day a follower peeped through the keyhole and saw him. For centuries after his death, people went on pilgrimages to his chapel among the hills of Perthshire.

A bone from the body of St Columba worked magic too, for it was able to halt the plague in the Dunkeld district. When people there were infected, the Bishop stirred this sacred relic in a bowl of water and each sick person drank from it. By all accounts, the potion had wonderful cures to its credit. In St Andrews too, at the ancient Norman church of St Rule, were three fingers, a tooth and a knee-cap from the skeleton of St Andrew, the patron saint of Scotland. Invalids even from far distant parts of England came to St Andrews to be cured by those

*The giant stag of the Canongate*
(From the Holyrood Abbey seal)

relics. So it was scarcely surprising that at Holyrood Abbey the True Cross had its miracles.

In the thirteenth century the number of religious buildings in and around Edinburgh was still growing. In 1230, King Alexander II arranged for Scotland's first Black Friars monastery to be built in the hollow to the south of the castle rock. This was never a wealthy foundation, for the Dominican friars had no worldly possessions. They went out among the people, preaching the word of God and depending on charity for the food they ate. But still their humble home became known as the King's Mansion, because Alexander II sometimes lived there. Though monasteries were not the most comfortable of houses, in one respect they were better than any royal palace. Even three centuries later not a single palace or castle in Scotland had a drainage system to compare with that of an average religious house in the thirteenth century. And sanitation was important for any king who travelled the countryside with a long train of courtiers.

Close to the Black Friars monastery another religious house was taking shape, the Church of St Mary-in-the-Field, later to be known as Kirk-o'-Field.

*St Margaret's Chapel and Mons Meg*

Holyrood Abbey too was growing in size and beauty, with a west front as handsome as almost any in Britain. Sculptured above the doorway can still be seen the seraphs in the heavenly choir that was carved at that time. Augustinian canons had taken over the running of the abbey and a little community was growing up nearby in what aptly became known as the Canongate, the canons' street. It was very much a village of churchmen, this tiny burgh of the Canongate. Though its canons never enjoyed trading rights to compare with those of their neighbours up the hill in Edinburgh, they at least got privileges that other villages without an abbey were never allowed.

*St Margaret's Chapel — the Chancel Arch*

Holyrood climbed the hill to pay homage to him there in St Margaret's Chapel. A few weeks later, further homage ceremonies were held — in the Chamber of the Blessed Margaret, which later became known as the King's Chamber. When he returned to England he took many of Scotland's treasures including the Black Rood. But he soon sent that one back.

Five years later a much less friendly King Edward led an army into Scotland to depose John Baliol, the King he had chosen on that previous visit. He arrived at Edinburgh on a Wednesday early in June and took up residence in Holyrood Abbey. Beside the Abbey he set up three of his catapults and soon huge boulders were soaring over the rooftops and pounding the castle day and night. By the fifth day it was badly damaged and the defenders were beginning to sue for peace. But the negotiations broke down. On the eighth day, as the end drew near, he went on to Linlithgow with most of his troops, while his catapults continued their bombardment. So the castle surrendered. Among the treasures then removed were "a shrine with the King of Scotland's arms, covered with red sinstone", silver cups, mazers and basins of various sizes, and crystal cups mounted in silver-gilt. These were never returned.

Within a few months Sir William Wallace had raised an army of liberation and the long-drawn-out Wars of Independence began. Not the least of Wallace's early worries was the loss of trade that the English invasion had brought to Leith and other Scottish ports. Until then this trade had been on an international scale. The ships of the Scottish merchants were familiar in ports all over Europe.

So in 1297 he wrote a letter from Haddington to the mayors of Lubeck and Hamburg, impressing on them that business had now returned to normal. The merchants of those two cities, he wrote, could again safely send their merchandise to all the ports of the Kingdom of Scotland, for — God be praised! — the land had now been re-covered by war from the English. But he wrote too soon.

From then almost until the eve of the battle of Bannockburn, Edinburgh Castle was in English hands. Then came its second tale of high adventure. All the important strongholds north of the Forth had surrendered to the Scottish forces, and this was the only strategic one still in foreign hands. When Earl Randolph, a nephew of King Robert the Bruce, laid siege to it, he found it too well defended and too well provisioned to fall easily. So he planned a surprise attack.

Among his men was a certain William Frances, who had been stationed there in happier and more romantic days. He used to slip out of his quarters and down the almost precipitous south face of the rock, to spend the nights with his sweetheart. Now, with his knowledge of this secret route, he led an assault force of thirty men in an attack on the castle. With their feet wrapped in rags to deaden their steps, and their swords dangling from slings around their necks, they carried short ladders with hooks on the end to get them over the parapet wall. The castle was captured almost before its English defenders were aware of their coming. In the destruction which followed, the only building spared was St Margaret's Chapel.

A few months later came the battle of Bannockburn but Scotland's troubles were still unsolved after that victory. In 1322 an English army overran the Lothians and sacked Holyrood Abbey. In 1337 they came again. For them the castle at Edinburgh had a strategic value, guarding the corridor between the Pentlands and the sea, one of the main routes into the heart of Scotland. So, that year, the English rebuilt the castle on the ruins that Randolph had left a quarter of a century before.

They might have saved themselves the trouble. One April day, only four years later, the castle's English governor was visited by the skipper of a merchant ship newly arrived at Leith — from England, he said, though he was in fact from

Dundee. He gave a mouth-watering description of his cargo — Rhenish wine and strong beer, with biscuits excellently spiced — and he offered the governor a generous share, free of charge, if he would turn a blind eye to the way the skipper disposed of the rest of the cargo. So, a few hours later, a long procession of mules, laden with barrels and sacks, came plodding up the High Street and on to the Castle Hill. Some of the mules were already across the drawbridge and inside the castle, when suddenly all their cargo toppled to the ground. Not only the approaches were blocked. The drawbridge itself was jammed. Then came the battle-cry "A Douglas! A Douglas!" and armed men stormed into the attack. All opposition was speedily swept aside and the castle was again destroyed, to prevent it being used by the English.

The Scots, however, were not always on the winning side. Five years later King David II was captured in a crushing defeat at Neville's Cross. Eleven years passed before he was ransomed back and one of the treasures he lost in the battle was never recovered. He had taken the Black Rood with him and it fell into the hands of the English. Given to Durham Cathedral, it stayed there until it finally disappeared at the Reformation.

# 3

## Groomed to be Capital

*In this drawing of Edinburgh Castle in 1560, King David's Tower can be seen on the left of St Margaret's Chapel.*

BY THE mid-fourteenth century Edinburgh was growing in size. And though the constant threat of English attack gave it little chance of ever becoming the capital of Scotland, it was already a town of some importance, one of the large burghs, with about four hundred houses.

It was even acquiring class barriers, for the burgesses were beginning to form themselves into two quite separate groups. There were the craftsmen who plied their trades — the bakers, the fleshers, fishmongers and skinners; the weavers who clothed their neighbours; the hammermen who fashioned all sorts of things from horses' shoes to swords and armour, and treasures in silver and gold; the wrights and masons who built the houses and cathedrals; and the barbers who could trim a most elegant beard or, in their surgeon branch, whip off a gangrenous leg with uncanny speed.

Quite apart from these were the merchants whose ships sailed from Leith

to the far ends of the great flat world. Buying and selling was their business and they acquired a wealth that the craftsmen could only envy. So, when kings needed to be ransomed back from England, it was the merchants who were most likely to have the necessary money. With their wealth the Edinburgh ones ruled the town. Only a merchant could become the Provost or a bailie, and the large majority of other councillors had to be merchants too.

When David II returned from exile, Edinburgh for the first time became the favourite residence of a King of Scotland. There was little comfort in the castle. Destroyed by Randolph and again by Sir William Douglas some thirty years later, it was mostly in ruins. King David, therefore, built a modern mansion on top of the castle rock. And a modern Scottish mansion — all through the Middle Ages — was one which went up and up, with no corridors but with narrow turnpike stairs leading from the basement to the lofty ramparts. In troubled times, stairs were much easier to defend than corridors.

The castle which David II built was by no means the first tower house in Scotland. Several others, oblong in shape, had been built elsewhere and can still be seen. But his was probably the first to display a new and even safer design, for his was L-shaped. King David's Tower, sixty feet high, dominated the skyline of the castle rock.

The work began in 1368 and three years later he died there. For the first time, the Royal Mile saw the funeral of a Scottish monarch, for until then Dunfermline Abbey had been their usual place of interment. David II's body was borne in state down to its burial beside the high altar in Holyrood Abbey. His tower house in the castle was still far from finished. The last stone was not laid until 1379.

Two years after his death, in the reign of Robert II a lucky thing happened to Edinburgh. During a peasants' revolt in England the Duke of Lancaster, John of Gaunt, took refuge for a time with the canons at Holyrood Abbey and for the rest of his life he never forgot the kindness he had received from them. So, when his King commanded him to lead a punitive raid into Scotland in 1384, he was troubled by his conscience.

When John of Gaunt's conscience troubled him, his reactions were different from those of lesser mortals. This time, ignoring the expectations of his King and the rage of his entire army, he let it be known that the people of the Lothians would get three full days to remove their goods and cattle over the Forth into the heart of Scotland, where they would be safe. His English troops were furious, for plunder was the acknowledged fruit of victory. But the householders of Edinburgh were delighted. Not content just to remove their furnishings, they even stripped off the thatched roofs of their houses and transported them into the forests beyond the Forth, to prevent them being set alight.

And, when you come to think of it, that was a strange thing to do — to take the roofs and leave the walls — if the walls of the houses of Edinburgh in those days were really built of wood.

That kindly raid, unfortunately, was merely a prelude to plunder postponed. All its good effect was spoiled by the unexpected arrival a few months later of John de Vienne, the Admiral of France, with a party of followers. He came for a sporting foray across the Border into England and by the laws of chivalry the Scottish King could hardly refuse such a reasonable request. But it was most inconvenient. Even Froissart, the French historian, admitted that many a Scotsman was asking why the devil those Frenchmen had come.

The outcome was that another English army marched north to sack Edinburgh.

As the enemy approached, the Scottish King offered housing sites inside the castle walls to the canons of Holyrood and the wealthiest of the Edinburgh burgesses. But there was little time for housebuilding. The English occupied the town

*The Edinburgh Tolbooth in the eighteenth century, with its medieval Bellhouse next to St Giles'.*

for five days and then began systematically to destroy it. Only the castle was left undamaged. Even the twelfth century Kirk of St Giles was damaged by fire and the Bellhouse was gutted.

Next year King Robert gave the townspeople a site twenty yards long and ten yards deep, on the north side of the street, to build a new Bellhouse. For more than a century the old one had been the very heart of the royal burgh. Every time there were goods to be sold at the market or meetings to be held on civic affairs, its bell rang out to summon the burgesses. That was where tolls were collected, where Council meetings and burgh courts were held, and wrongdoers and debtors and the mentally deranged imprisoned.

Every Scottish burgh had its Bellhouse. Usually the old name was eventually dropped and it became known as the Tolbooth instead. This happened in Edinburgh too. But there the eastern end,

the most handsome part, never lost its medieval name of Bellhouse.

There was more peace with England after that and soon the pattern of trade began to change. For over a century there had been an English stranglehold on Leith. Almost all the Continental shipping had shunned that port and moved north to the safer havens of Fife and Angus. But now the centre of commerce was moving south again, back to Leith, and the little port was scarcely able to cope with so much trade.

In 1398 the Lord of Restalrig, Sir Robert Logan, gave some of his land along the shore for harbour improvements. A bridge was built over the Water of Leith to provide an easier approach to the quayside, and the quays themselves were extended to give more space for loading and unloading. Fifteen years later the need was still growing, and again the merchants went to Sir Robert for more ground where they could

store their cargoes. In 1424 King James I was ransomed back to Scotland after eighteen years in England. As some compensation for the merchants who had paid his ransom, one of his first actions was to let them impose a toll on all ships using the port, to pay for still more improvements.

Wines were among the chief imports then and hides the chief exports. Two members of Edinburgh's Town Council made sure that the imported wines arrived in good condition, while four others kept a check on the carcases that were slaughtered for export.

*    *    *

Normally, in those days, the centre of a town was not a street but a market place and what we now know as the Royal Mile was in fact wider than today.

At this stage perhaps we should still assume that the houses overlooking the market place were all of wood. And yet there are some niggling doubts about that. We have already seen that in 1384 the burgesses carried off their thatched roofs, to prevent them being burned by English invaders, and it is hard to believe that the walls they left were also of wood. Aeneas Sylvius came to Scotland in 1435 and made a comment no less strange — that most of the houses in the towns were constructed with lime. But, whether those along the High Street of Edinburgh were wooden or stone-built, at that time anyway they witnessed one of the most gruesome spectacles ever seen in any Christian country.

Only a year after the visit by Aeneas Sylvius, King James I was murdered, and soon crowds came flocking into the High Street to see the blood-chilling tortures and hangings that followed. The Earl of Atholl was one of the guilty men. Wearing only a loin cloth he was tossed in the air and dragged along the causeway back and forth, time after time, and then a crown of red-hot iron was placed on his head. So ended the first day with him still alive. On the second day he was tied to a horse's tail and dragged through the surrounding villages. On the third day he lived just long enough to be disembowelled before he died. But the worst punishment was reserved for Robert Stewart, the chief conspirator. His went down in history.

It was a gruesome age. When the new King, James II, was only ten years old he attended a banquet given in Edinburgh Castle by Sir William Crichton, the Chancellor of Scotland. The guests included the young Earl of Douglas and his brother. In those days the over-mighty Douglas lords travelled the countryside with a retinue as large as any king's. And this time the two brothers, fearing treachery, were not content with just an army of followers. They also had a promise of safe conduct from Sir William.

Although the followers were able to go only as far as the castle drawbridge, the two brothers felt safe enough inside. They were warmly welcomed by Sir William and in the great hall the company "banquetted royally with all delicates which could be got". Then, despite the tears and entreaties of the boy King, the Douglases were dragged from the hall to their death on the Castle Hill. Even in that age of violence their murder caused widespread horror, commemorated in a famous ballad —

> Edinburgh Castle, toune and toure,
> God grant thou sink for sinne!
> And that even for the black dinoir
> Earl Douglas gat therein.

It was not the kind of crime that the Douglases could easily forgive or forget. Edinburgh saw much of them during the next year, for they rallied their followers and besieged the castle for nine months, until Sir William surrendered.

Edinburgh by then had a new loch. It had always had one on its southern side where the Meadows now are, and on this South Loch it long depended for its water supply. But for the loch on its northern side, in the hollow now occupied by Princes Street Gardens, it had to thank the military advisers of the child king

James II. Scarcely two years after he came to the throne, the English were mustering again after three-quarters of a century of uneasy peace, and an attack on Edinburgh seemed imminent. Fearing that it might come from the north, the defenders dammed the small Craig Burn which flowed through the hollow, and the overflow became a broad defensive moat. The threat soon vanished. The English army was routed at the Sark. But the Nor' Loch continued to fill the hollow for the next four centuries.

In spite of internal violence and threats of foreign invasion, life in Edinburgh went on undisturbed. You might almost say that already the town was being groomed for its future role as the capital of Scotland. To preserve law and order, the first really stringent licensing laws were introduced by Parliament. Each night the ringing of the curfew bell in the Bellhouse tower became a signal that the door of every tavern in the town must be closed. That prevented many a drunken frolic by night. Six years later, as a further safeguard, the old custom was revived of locking the burgh gates between curfew-time and 5 a.m. You had to pay for admission between those hours — a penny for ordinary folk and twice as much for "the best of the town", who could more easily afford it.

Other changes too were on the way. Shopkeeping was coming into vogue. But only the most influential burgesses could hope to have booths of their own, for space was limited. The Bellhouse, the hub of the town's commercial life, was the only place where booths were allowed. Soon there were six along its south wall, two along its west wall and five under the Bellhouse stair. Other six were inside the building, five of them actually in the Tolbooth chamber. All through the next quarter-of-a-century the number remained at twenty-two. The rest of the burgesses had to be content to trade in the traditional way round the market cross, where the townspeople had done their buying and selling from time immemorial.

There was not just one market but fifteen, each assigned to its own traditional stance. Only one of them had to be outside the town — the cattle mart on the western outskirts at the King's Stables. The sale of live cattle inside the town was forbidden.

Close to the Belltower and the Kirk of St Giles, poultry was on sale beside the market cross. There you could buy "partrikis, pluuaris, capons, conyngis, chekinnis and all uther wyld fowlis and tame". For a pair of shoes you had to go farther up the street to the cordiners' market, which stretched uphill from just opposite the Bellhouse. If you wanted ordinary shoes you probably bought three instead of a pair, for they were made to fit either foot and three was economical. The cordiners' high-sounding name came from the Spanish city of Cordova, famed for its goatskin leather.

Farther uphill was the meal market, reaching as far as Liberton's Wynd. Beyond that, at the Over Bow, was the market for dairy produce, wool and other goods that had to be weighed. So the upper trone was there — one of the two great balances that the town provided for goods sold by weight. Beyond that again was the Lawnmarket, where cotton and linen cloth was sold.

Downhill from the Bellhouse, on the north side of the street, were the removable krames (or stalls) of the chapmen. And across from them on the south side the hatmakers and skinners faced each other. In those days a hide often served as a door for a but-and-ben, and thus many a countryman went to the skinners' market when he needed a new door for his cottage. But leather generally had a much wider variety of uses than now.

Beyond the chapmen, the hatmakers and the skinners was the lower trone, close beside where the Tron Church now is. Here again there was much coming and going with goods to be weighed, for the meat market and the fishmarket were just beyond. The meat stands stretched from the trone to Blackfriars Wynd and the fishmarket from the Friars' Wynd to

*The North Loch, drawn by Captain John Slezer in the late 17th century, when the high flats of Edinburgh were at their highest.*

the Netherbow. If you wanted to pickle your purchase, you could get your salt in Niddry's Wynd nearby.

Still farther down, beyond the Netherbow and especially around St Mary's Wynd, the various branches of the Hammermen — the cutlers, lockmakers, smiths and lorimers — offered their work for sale.

Most of the burgesses owned a horse or two. For their feeding stuffs they went down to the Cowgate, to the part between the foot of Foresters' Wynd and Peebles Wynd. Nearer to the new-built Grey Friars monastery but in the same district was the timber market. Yet another market, more familiar on the Continent than in Scotland, a market for "ald graith and geir", was probably introduced by the Grey Friars from Cologne. This second-hand market was held on Fridays in front of the Grey Friars monastery, "lyke as is vsit in vthir cuntreis".

It was in 1447 that the brown-robed Grey Friars came to Edinburgh. Their monastery was already built for them before they arrived and they had merely to move in. Overlooking the Grassmarket and almost opposite the West Bow, it stood at the north end of what is now the graveyard, fully a hundred feet west of the burial yett at the foot of the Candlemaker Row. But then there was no burial ground and it seemed for a time there would be no Grey Friars monastery either. The house prepared for them on the King's instructions was so magnificent that when Cornelius of Zurick See arrived with his friars he took one look at it and refused to move in. For Franciscans, he said, it was far too grand. A vast amount of persuading was needed before he reluctantly changed his mind.

\* \* \*

Edinburgh by then was very near to being the capital of Scotland. But it had never been a walled town and it was just too prone to attack. In 1450 James II took steps to remedy that. He allowed the inhabitants "to fosse, bulwark, wall, toure, turate and uther wais to strengthen oure forsaids Burgh", because "thai dreid the evil and skeith of our ennemies of England".

The wall is said to have run from the Wellhouse Tower in Princes Street Gardens to a point opposite the Castle Hill reservoir, then over the hill to the middle of the West Bow and east behind Parliament House to the Mint Close and the Nether Bow. And certainly part of it can still be seen, running west from the lower bend of the West Bow and forming the base of the passageway above Dewar's Close. The most impressive part is below St Columba's Church and the Public Health Department building in Johnston Terrace, where it is complete with buttresses.

It is by no means certain, however, that this was the wall of 1450. Nothing in the civic records suggests that any wall was built that year or even in 1473, when James III told the Council to build one. The records are silent about any town wall until a year after Flodden. And so we can be fairly sure that the part still visible below Johnston Terrace is not a fragment of a 1450 wall but of the much earlier King's Wall, mentioned in several old documents long before Flodden as a boundary of properties.

When it was first built, this wall may have enclosed the whole town. By the mid-fifteenth century, however, it no longer did so. The new Grey Friars monastery and the iron-work market at St Mary's Wynd were both outside the wall. So were half the dead in the burial ground beside the Kirk of St Giles. There the wall circled the hillside, halfway down, splitting the churchyard in two.

Also outside the wall was the Cowgate, soon to become the most fashionable street in Edinburgh. As early as 1438, mansions were already being built there.

Not everyone thought Cowgate a suitable name for such an elegant new thoroughfare. Even as late as 1480 it was still being called South Street by some and Well-gait by others because public and private wells were there. No one, of course, was worried about having to live

outside the wall. There is scant evidence that any Edinburgh wall ever kept out a hostile army that wanted in.

During the reign of James II the town got its first recreation park. It too was outside the wall, at the east end of the new North Loch. Even recreation in those days had a martial air. Tournaments and other warlike sports were what the King had in mind in 1456, when he gave the burgesses this land of Greenside, between the Calton Hill on the east and the earthen road to Leith on the west.

People, however, were not always thinking of war. Among the more light-hearted occasions was New Year's Day, which had already supplanted Christmas as the highlight of the festive season. That was a time when troubles and class distinctions were all forgotten. Even the King took part in those annual frolics. After morning mass and the usual exchange of presents at the castle, he abdicated to let the King of the Bean take over for the next few hours. The new sovereign was not always a courtier. Once, indeed, a trumpeter in the castle guard was chosen.

Throughout the year there was pomp and ceremony too. Parliament was now meeting in Edinburgh far more often than ever before. A royal decree of 1454 added to the burgh's prestige. From then on, the annual meetings of the Court of Parliament were held there. In almost everything but name, Edinburgh had become the capital of Scotland. It had become uncommonly religious too.

# 4

## Back to Religion

*The Church of the Holy Trinity beside the North Loch*

IT WAS a long time since Edinburgh had possessed any miraculous relic. Over a century had passed since the Black Rood fell into the hands of the English. Holyrood Abbey too had lost its fragment of the True Cross. But now came the exciting news that one of the leading townsmen, William Preston of Goirton, had brought home from France a genuine arm-bone of St Giles. It had cost him a vast sum of money and he would never have been able to buy it if the King of France had not used his influence in the final stages.

Mr Preston died in 1454 and left the relic to the Kirk of St Giles with three conditions attached. When it was carried in procession, it was to be borne by his nearest kinsman. Within six or seven years an aisle was to be built to house it. And a chaplain was to be appointed who, for the next five years, would sing masses for the soul of the donor.

Mr Preston was buried in the Lady Aisle and adjoining it a new aisle was built as a shrine for the sacred relic. No expense was spared. With its three bays and its groined roof in the Gothic style, this Preston Aisle was one of the most beautiful in Britain. Other improvements were carried out too. The choir was enlarged and the central roof raised to

form a clerestory. By 1462 the work was finished.

Of all the miracles that the arm-bone produced, by far the greatest was a sudden upsurge of religion in the town. The wealthy merchants and the humblest craftsmen were all infected. Soon every craft wanted to erect an altar in the parish church in honour of its particular patron saint.

The Shoemakers seem to have been first with their altar of St Crispin in 1449, when William Preston was still alive. But the Skinners may have been earlier. Certainly they had one by 1450, for in that year at a meeting in the Church of St Mary-in-the-Field they bound each member to contribute according to his means, for the duration of his life, to support a chaplain and repair the ornaments "of the altar of St Christopher lately founded" by them. By 1456 the Bakers had an altar of St Ubertis.

In 1475 we hear of the Masons and Wrights holding daily services at their altar of St John the Evangelist. A much wealthier craft than the Shoemakers, the Skinners or the Bakers, they had taken over the aisle of St John the Baptist, of which Sir John Scaithmure had previously been patron. The Weavers maintained the altar of St Severan, while the Wakers had an altar of St Mark, Philip and Jacob.

Wealthiest of all were the Hammermen. Like the Masons and Wrights, they had a chapel of their own, containing their altar of St Eloi. Long ago the altar disappeared but the Hammermen's little chapel still survives near the north door of the church. The Fleshers, the Hatmakers and the Coopers had their altars too.

Oddly enough, breaking the rules of the craft was as good a way as any to ensure that the chaplain would never be short of candles. If you broke the rules, disobeyed your deacon, enticed an apprentice away from his master, or failed to pay your penny each Monday as a booth-holder, you paid for your sin with one or two pounds of wax for the altar candles. But there were money payments too, towards the upkeep of the altar and its chaplain. The weekly pennies went there. So did the apprentices' entry fees, which ranged from five shillings upwards, and the much larger fees on completion of the apprenticeship. The Seals of Cause of the various crafts — the rules they drew up for their members — are studded with references to those altars.

Life was exciting then. The wealth of the town was growing and the stonemasons were busier than ever before, for the High Street was changing. Stone-built houses had become very fashionable. And those houses were solidly built. Many of them survived three hundred years and more. Beside "John Knox's House" in the High Street is the still older Mowbray House. Parts of it still survive that were built at this time, well over five centuries ago, and that is a good old age for any domestic building in a town.

At Edinburgh Castle the builders were busy too, putting the finishing touches to another of James II's defensive plans. Like most Stuart kings he was passionately fond of weapons of war and the most regal of all such weapons was undoubtedly the new artillery. Only a king could afford such luxury.

For well over a century there had been guns of sorts in the castle. King Robert II. the first of the royal collectors, paid four pounds in 1384 for a little "instrument called a gun". In 1430 James I more ambitiously sent to Flanders for "an enormous bombard".

Cannons, you might say, formed the guard of honour at the wedding of James II, for his bride's marriage portion included guns from the famous Flemish foundries. But he had more than a collector's interest. The artillery was part of his defensive plan. Having a town wall, a defensive moat, and a tournament ground where his officers could train was not enough. In the castle, beside King David's Tower, a gun platform was erected. From the gun-loops of this platform, all through the next century,

C

*The castle guns of James II menaced not only the enemy*

six cannons were ready to roar defiance at any invading force that might come marching up the High Street.

It was awkward, of course, for the burgesses, their wives and children. Old writers love to tell how the townsfolk built their houses in the friendly shelter of the castle walls, knowing that there they were safe. But it wasn't quite like that, after the gun-platforms were erected. The guns menaced not only the enemy. Every house along the street was in the line of fire and liable to be blown sky-high. Yet it was the King himself who had most cause to regret his passion for artillery. In his earlier years he was described as "over-curious in the matter of engines of war". Now he went off with some of them to besiege the English garrison in Roxburgh Castle. One of his cannons "brak in the fyring" and killed him.

The body of the 29-year-old King was brought back to Holyrood Abbey for burial. He had succeeded to the throne at the age of six. Now the country had another child king, the nine-year-old James III.

There were signs by then that religion was changing, not only in Edinburgh but in Scotland as a whole. For centuries Roman Catholicism had been largely monastic but now the ordinary folk were determined to become more personally involved. Even the priests, no longer content to lead a life apart, were going out among the people as they had never done before. The old parish churches were being changed into collegiate churches, the focal points in this new crusading venture.

In 1467 the Kirk of St Giles ceased to be an ordinary parish church and became a Collegiate Church instead, with a provost, a dean, sixteen prebendaries, a master of the choir and four choristers, a sacristan and a beadle, as well as all the chaplains in attendance at the altars. But

*Queen Mary of Gueldres returns as an angel to play the medieval organ in her Church of the Holy Trinity. In the background is the apse, the only part of the building which survives.*

*The numbers can still be seen on many of the stones, on the
walls of the reading room at the foot of Chalmers Close.*

*The Church of the Holy Trinity in the mid-eighteenth century.*

this was not the first of Edinburgh's collegiate churches. There was another that the Queen Mother, Mary of Gueldres, had erected about five years earlier in memory of her dead husband, James II. Close to the North Loch, this Church of the Holy Trinity was one of the most beautiful ever built in Edinburgh. Through it she hoped to gain the salvation of the Kings and Queens of Scotland and the forgiveness "of all whom in her lifetime she had in any way offended".

The church was never completed. She died about a year after the work began and only the choir, the central tower and the cross were finished, with an old folk's home for thirteen bedesmen. But what was finished was full of the pride of craftsmanship.

Some idea of its richness can be gained from four exquisite panels which once adorned the high altar. One of these shows the interior of the church as it was in medieval times, and Mary of Gueldres

herself is said to be the angel playing the organ. In front kneels Sir Edward Bonkil, first provost of the church. The organ, specially made in Flanders, was a gift from him in 1467. From Flanders too came the distinguished artist Hugo van der Goes, who painted this Trinity altarpiece between 1467 and 1475.

Mary of Gueldres was dead by then. She was buried in the north aisle of her church four years before the provost installed his organ. Her son James III and her grandson James IV are depicted on another of the panels, while yet another shows her daughter-in-law Margaret of Denmark, the Queen of James III. All those panels now have a place of honour in the National Galleries of Scotland.

The church itself no longer exists. In 1848 it was demolished to let the Waverley Station be built. But people were sentimental about the lovely old church. They carefully numbered all the stones in readiness for its re-erection on another site. Sites unfortunately seem to

C*

*On top is a statue of St Triduana.*

have been hard to find at the middle of last century. The stones remained heaped in a great pile on the Calton Hill until 1871, when the work at last began, close to the original site, at the foot of Chalmers Wynd. Many of the stones had disappeared by then and only enough were left to rebuild the handsome old apse. Now a newspaper reading room run by the Corporation of Edinburgh, it has many of the numbers still clearly visible on its outer walls.

There is another reminder of the pious Queen Mary of Gueldres, in another collegiate church, built in her lifetime. Beside the present parish church of Restalrig, until some seventy years ago, you could still see the scattered ruins of a much older building. This too was a collegiate church, destroyed at the Reformation. When restoration work began in 1907, a finely carved boss with the arms of the Queen was discovered. But whether she was responsible for the building of this church is uncertain. The arms of the Logans who owned the lands of Restalrig were also found.

There was an old tradition that the ruins were those of the chapterhouse and it was obvious that the building had been two storeys high. When the work began, the ground was littered with fragments of vaulting from the upper storey. But this "upper chapel", as it was described in a deed of 1477, was too badly damaged to be rebuilt. The restoration had to be concentrated on the lower hall with its central pillar and groin vaulting.

[38]

*St Triduana's Well, soon after it was rediscovered.*

Right from the start the workmen had trouble from rising water. When they tried to lay a concrete floor, the water came bubbling through in jets. They tried a thick layer of asphalt and soon it was completely destroyed. In the end they used large paving stones with heavy boulders on top, leaving only a sump covered by an iron plate. Some workmen were standing on this, one day, when the plate and the men were suddenly hurled in all directions.

Then for the first time it was realised that this was no chapterhouse — that the hall beneath the chapel was in fact the long-lost Well of St Triduana, famed in

*St Margaret's Well before the stonework*
*was removed last century.*

the Middle Ages for its miraculous cures of eye troubles.

It was not the only holy well in Restalrig. There was another with an even stranger story. Called St Margaret's Well, it stood on a mossy bank that sloped down to a pleasant meadow. In the late Middle Ages it too was enclosed by an elaborate stone shrine, very like St Triduana's but much smaller. It too had a central pillar, a rib-vaulted roof and decorative bosses. But it was only about a quarter the size of the other and obviously a little later in date.

St Margaret's Well had an ideal situation. Standing in its doorway you breathed in the fresh air, as you watched the overflow rippling gently across the meadow. But all things must change.

About the end of the eighteenth century the problems of Edinburgh were growing fast, so the pleasant meadow became a foul-smelling morass, where the sewage from the town's open drains was dumped. If you had gone in those days to be healed at the holy well, you would have done so at your peril.

Later came the North British Railway with its engine sheds. A great complex of buildings replaced the sewage farm and St Margaret's Well disappeared from sight, though in fact it was still there. From outside the new buildings a doorway led into an inky black passage, long and vaulted, which led through the darkness to the ornate well. It was like going into the bowels of the earth. In 1859, after a storm of protest, most of the

stonework was removed and rebuilt on the north slope of Salisbury Crags beside a spring that was known as St David's Well.

Those two wells at Restalrig, built in the reigns of James II and James III, had no parallel in Scotland. Though in those days there were hundreds of healing wells, in all parts of the country, nowhere else were there any with shrines as magnificent as these.

*       *       *

Edinburgh by then was changing for the better. Only a century before, an English nobleman had called it "a mean place". Now, in 1478, another Englishman thought it "a most wealthy town". The new religious buildings were not the only ones which gave it this air of opulence. The merchants and the master craftsmen had an air of prosperity too.

Not everyone in those days was allowed to set up a workshop and embark on a trade. Weavers and hatmakers had to serve a five-years' apprenticeship and in most trades it was seven years instead of five. Even when that was finished, promotion to the rank of craftsman was by no means automatic. A rigorous examination by a panel of experts decided whether you had acquired the necessary skill. If you failed and were still fairly young, your apprenticeship could be lengthened to give you another chance. If you were older, you had to spend the rest of your days as an employee with no hope of ever becoming a master craftsman.

The successful ones, having paid their fee to become freemen, could then start in a workshop of their own. But they were still not entirely their own masters. To ensure that they were always a credit to their craft, their work was liable to be inspected at any time. Every day, the deacon of the fleshers went on his rounds to see that no diseased animal was killed for sale. You could be banished from the town for that. Though the penalties for skinners were less severe, they too could be fined for selling sheepskins that had been carelessly damaged.

To become a master weaver you had not only to prove your own skill. Your looms and other equipment had to be capable of turning out work of quality. In those days of high fashion there was always a demand for fine cloths that were locally made, though the best were still imported. Fine craftsmanship was needed too, if you wanted to become a tailor to the nobility who now had their town houses in Edinburgh. This needed a seven-years' apprenticeship. Making fine shoes needed seven years too.

The Hammerman craft was another where the search for quality went on unendingly. Every Saturday morning three experts went round to ensure that all work on display was "sufficient in stuff and workmanship, gude worth and hable work to serve the Kingis liegis". Selling faulty goods was a serious offence.

There were various kinds of Hammermen — blacksmiths, saddlers, cutlers, armourers and goldsmiths, with the goldsmiths wealthiest of all. Each had to stick to his own particular branch of the craft. But they were not over-troubled by outside competition. Except for four hours on market day, no one was allowed to sell imported goods that the Hammermen of Edinburgh could have made themselves.

The most rigid of all the checks were on the masons and wrights, for lives could be lost if their work was faulty. Two expert masons and wrights made sure at every stage that the work was "lelely and treulie done". And if this expert advice was ignored the Town Council was the final arbiter.

In 1482 King Edward IV of England described Edinburgh as "that right fair and opulent city". But one new building, erected then in the heart of the town, was by no means fair. For three centuries it stood in the High Street as an indispensable part of its commercial life, and all through those centuries it was being condemned as an eyesore. It was built

because the very small number of booths that were then available had become a grievance to merchants and craftsmen alike. Freemen were beginning to set up their own booths, out in the street or under the stairs of their houses. To stop that, the Luckenbooths — the locked booths — were built, uncomfortably close to the Kirk of St Giles. They grew in size over the years, until eventually they stretched the whole length of the church, with room for only a narrow footpath between. And they contrasted oddly with its rich decorations, for the Luckenbooths were by no means a thing of beauty. The passage between the two became known in its earliest days as the Stinking Style and that name stuck through the centuries.

But it really was an excellent site for a supermarket. And, when you bore in mind all the money that the craftsmen were paying then, to maintain the altars and chaplains in the Collegiate Kirk of St Giles, it would have been churlish to think they should take their Luckenbooths elsewhere.

While the craftsmen were getting their booths, the castle was having another of its moments of high drama. Treason was in the air, with the barons on the verge of open revolt against James III. Even the King's brothers — the Earl of Mar and the Duke of Albany — fell under suspicion. In 1479 he had them thrown into prison.

When Mar died mysteriously in Craigmillar Castle, the rumour spread like wildfire that he had been murdered by the King. Albany was in Edinburgh Castle, in King David's Tower, and soon people were saying that he was next on the list.

One day two casks of malvoisie were delivered to him from a ship newly arrived at Leith. In one was a coil of rope and a message that he must escape without delay, down the north side of the castle rock, for the King's minions had resolved that he should die ere the morrow's sun had set.

That night Albany invited the captain of the guard and three of the officers to join him in sampling the wine over dinner. He made them half-drunk, stabbed them to death and flung their bodies on the open fire, where "in their armour they broiled and sweltered like tortoises in iron shells". Then the perilous escape down the rock face began. Too late he found that the escape rope was not long enough. His page, going first, fell from the end of it and broke his thigh. Albany then lengthened the rope with blankets and, reaching the ground in safety, carried his page all the way to Leith, where a ship was waiting to take them out of the country.

By a strange twist of fate, only three years later James III was himself a prisoner in the castle, with his nobles in revolt, and it was Albany who rescued him with the help of the burgesses of Edinburgh. The trouble flared up because the King chose his favourite Robert Cochran to be Earl of Mar and Secretary of State. Cochran was an intellectual, as well as a master mason at a time when building was among the most honourable of crafts. But, in the eyes of the barons, heredity was all that mattered. So they hanged Cochran at the Bridge of Lauder, and the King took refuge in Edinburgh Castle lest he should be hanged as well. The townspeople, led by the Duke of Albany, managed to drive off the besieging nobles and set him free.

James III never forgot his debt to the burgesses. That year, when he gave them a charter extending their trading privileges, he expressly referred to the courage they had shown in "exposing their persons to great peril of life, while besieging the said Castle, in consequence of which attack our royal person now rejoices in liberty".

It was the merchants who reaped the benefit of those new trading privileges. But the craftsmen are said to have been remembered too with a gift they treasured through the ages — the famous Blue Blanket. It must be admitted that, according to one eighteenth century writer, this Tradesmen's Banner existed

long before that. It was the Banner of the Holy Ghost, he said. A great regiment of Scottish craftsmen took it with them on a crusade to Palestine in the reign of William the Lion. But most folk agree that it was in fact gifted by the grateful James III. Tradition says that he handed it over personally at a ceremony in the Hammermen's Chapel, after the Queen and her ladies had decorated it with a Saltire or St Andrew's Cross, a thistle, an imperial crown and a hammer. The Queen herself embroidered the words:

Fear God and honour the King
With a long life and a prosperous reign,
And we that are Trades shall ever pray
To be faithful for the defence of his
    sacred Majesty's royal person till death.

For three centuries the Blue Blanket remained the symbol of all the rights that were exclusive to the burgess craftsmen of Edinburgh. They took it to Flodden and the blood-stained survivors brought it safely home. They flourished it in the face of James VI to remind him that not even he had a divine right to question their craftsmanship. And so the King angrily wrote in his "Basilicon Doros" that "the craftsmen think we should be content with their work, how bad and dear soever it be, and if they in anything be controlled, up goeth the blue blanket".

In the mid-eighteenth century the banner was still being displayed, every time the Deacon Convener and his Court sat in judgment on any craft dispute. When William Maitland was writing his history of Edinburgh in 1753, people still maintained that when the Deacon Convener brought out the blanket not only the craftsmen of Edinburgh but of all Scotland were obliged to follow him to battle. Possession of the banner made him chief craftsman of the whole country.

You can still see the historic banner, hanging on the wall of an upstairs gallery in the National Museum of Antiquities. Though faded with age, it is still recognisable with its pale blue background and the darker horizontal bars which gave it its name. A Lord Provost of Edinburgh put it into the Museum for safe keeping in 1850. And yet something is missing. There is not a trace of the Saltire and other emblems, or the inscription which Queen Margaret worked so lovingly five centuries ago. Perhaps the original banner was flourished too often. Perhaps it just couldn't last forever. Anyway, it disappeared long ago. No one can say how often a replacement had to be made over the years, but the one in the Museum was not the last of the line. It too was replaced in the late seventeenth century by a new silken banner, complete with all the trimmings, the Saltire, the emblems and the royal inscription. The dye on this one has faded from blue to pale green but the banner still survives, in the Trades Maidens Hospital in Melville Street.

Less than six years after the craftsmen got their original banner, James III met a violent death. His barons rose against him in 1488 and so he "happened to be slain". His fifteen-year-old son became King.

# 5

## Age of Splendour

JAMES IV was in many ways the greatest of the Stuart kings. Nine years after his reign began, a graphic description of him was sent to the King and Queen of Spain by their ambassador, the Marquis Don Pedro de Ayala.

The King, he wrote, was of noble stature and as handsome as a man could be. A very agreeable conversationalist with a wonderful knowledge of languages, he spoke Latin, French, German, Flemish, Italian and Spanish as well as his own Scotch language, which was as different from English as Aragonese from Castilian. He also spoke Gaelic, "the language of the savages who live in some parts of Scotland and in the islands". As for his Spanish, he was not only as fluent as the Marquis himelf but his pronunciation was better.

His piety was no less impressive. On Wednesdays and Fridays he ate no meat and on Sundays he never rode on horseback, even when going to mass. But his masses were by no means confined to Sundays, for he made a point of hearing two, before he would contract any business. He had a great liking for priests and especially for the Grey Friars, with whom he confessed.

Another trait unusual in kings was the fact that even in joking he seldom said anything that was not true. "He prides himself upon it," wrote Don Pedro, "and says it does not seem to him well for kings to swear their treaties as they do now. The oath of a king should be his royal word, as it was in bygone days."

A high State official of England, on seeing him for the first time on the eve of his wedding, thought "hys bearde somthynge long". That was scarcely surprising, for in all his life he cut neither his hair nor his beard. But de Ayala thought it became him very well.

This Spanish ambassador was not the only person who loved the King almost to the point of idolatry. He was one of the most popular of kings, a man who could mix with all men. And he never repeated his father's mistake of pursuing the arts to the exclusion of all else. He could shoot with the long bow, the crossbow and the hand-culverin. Among his favourite sports were tennis, "lang bowlis" and wildfowling. And he didn't need to go far from Edinburgh for his wildfowl. Four boatmen used to raise them on Lochend Loch, when he went hawking there. He was a golfer too, in those days when you could buy a dozen balls for twenty old pence and new clubs for fivepence each.

He liked horses and dogs even better than books, and his energy was tremendous. On one occasion he rode his white courser from Stirling to Aberdeen and on to Elgin in a single day. A certain restlessness in his nature kept him constantly on the move, from one end of his kingdom to the other. It gave him an understanding of his people that few of his advisers possessed.

There are all sorts of endearing stories about him. Because a mason had lost his job at Falkland Palace, he gave him fourteen shillings, a considerable sum in those days. A blind man by the roadside got the same amount and so did a countryman standing disconsolate beside his dead horse. He paid the surgeon's fee and other expenses, when the son of the

*Sitting ducks were less plentiful when James IV went wildfowling on Lochend Loch.*

*The Lantern Spire of the Kirk of St Giles*

royal chef broke his leg. "The puir wif on the gait that criit on the King" did not call in vain, and the man whose corn was trodden down by the royal horses got full compensation.

He lived, of course, in more exciting times than our dull age. Just four years after he ascended the throne, Christopher Columbus set sail from Spain with three ships and a combined crew of eighty-eight men, to discover America. Five years later Vasco da Gama sailed south round the newly discovered Cape of Good Hope to find a new route to India. And these lands were brimming over with untold riches, not dust like the moon. In Rome Leonardo da Vinci had just finished his greatest masterpiece, "The Last Supper". The churches of Italy were proudly buying each new Madonna by Raphael. And Michelangelo was already at the height of his fame. Very soon the scaffolding would be going up for him to start his grandest work, the ceiling of the Sistine Chapel. Architects were busy too, designing palaces and cathedrals in the new Renaissance style. St Peter's in Rome was among the finest of these. Its foundation stone was laid in 1508. But wherever you turned there was excitement in the air.

Pope Alexander VI must have liked James IV of Scotland. In 1494 he sent him a sceptre, richly decorated with a Madonna and Child. It was one of the few graven images which survived the Scottish Reformation. Perhaps it had a special immunity because it had become part of the regalia used at the coronation of the Kings of Scotland.

The Kirk of St Giles was growing fast, at the time when the sceptre arrived in Edinburgh. For three years there had been little peace in the High Street, for the masons and wrights began their work at five in the morning and didn't finish until seven at night, all through the summer months. In winter the din went on from dawn to dusk. And still the work was far from finished.

In 1495 they completed one ambitious part, the Albany Aisle at the north-west corner of the nave. There, on top of a finely fluted pillar, you can still see the arms of this Duke of Albany, Governor of Scotland and uncle of the King. We met him fifteen years before, when his guards were broiling and sweltering like tortoises in Edinburgh Castle.

Not only the Albany Aisle was built at the end of the fifteenth century. So was another part of St Giles' that has been a landmark ever since — the magnificent lantern spire with its delicate arches and fretted pinnacles, soaring above the finely fluted balustrade. The masons had good cause to be specially proud of that.

Folk in those days, however, were not obsessed only with godliness. They liked other things too. One day in July 1497 they gathered thick along the High Street, when the King's artillery was dragged out of the castle and down the street, past the church, en route for the siege of Norham just across the Border. There were horses and drivers by the hundreds, with sixty-one quarriers and masons, as well as wrights and smiths and a cooper in charge of the gunpowder barrels. Hundreds of labourers were also there, with their shovels and picks, to carve a road for the guns. It was a kingly display. Not even the wealthiest barons could afford such luxury. And even by kingly standards this was very special. Few monarchs in Europe had guns to compare with those in Edinburgh Castle. England had nothing like them.

Biggest of all those great weapons of war was Mons Meg. Forged in the Low Countries, she remained for centuries one of the biggest guns in the world. That day she had her own escort of musicians, as she rumbled triumphantly down the hill. The Exchequer gave the minstrels fourteen shillings for their pains. She had her own team of workmen too — a hundred of them plus five wrights and smiths who cost the king £32 a week. Though this was Scots money, the £ Scots was still worth 6s 8d in the English money of those days and vastly more than the £ sterling today.

There were other giant guns too in that

*Mons Meg, greatest of the King's guns and for centuries one of the largest in Europe.*

great parade but Mons Meg took pride of place — until just beyond the Abbey her cradle collapsed after one mighty jolt and her barrel crashed on the roadway. It took seven wrights almost three days to fashion a new and strong enough cradle for her to journey on.

As the procession lumbered southwards it gathered reinforcements of guns and oxen. By the middle of August it reached Norham and soon the artillery was thundering at the bishop's castle. Each day for a week James IV was in the thick of the fray, personally directing the gunfire. Each night he unwound over a game of cards with de Ayala. After seven days of the blasting gunfire, "how so be it, he did noo hurt to the castell".

But some hurt was coming to Edinburgh. People in those days were very broad-minded and, soon after the guns came back, the virulent French pox began to reach epidemic proportions. One September morning the sick were lined up on the sands of Leith and ferried across to the isle of Inchkeith, to stay there until God restored their health. Anyone with pox who ignored the summons was branded on the cheek with a red-hot iron and banished for ever from the town.

That was not the worst. Six months later the much more dreaded plague broke out in the surrounding hamlets and threatened the town. It was confirmed in Swanston and Currie, "Under Cramond" and Hailes. For people who lived there, it was tempting to flee to the shelter of some relative's house in Edinburgh. But that was one sure way to spread the disease, so the penalty was death. By the end of the year, Edinburgh was in a

state of siege with every close and back wall guarded day and night against intruders.

All through the winter the plague continued, while a frantic search went on to find the cause. Wool and skins came under suspicion and these were destroyed unless they came from a plague-free area. Dogs and swine — and children from infected houses — were an even greater danger. Every stray dog or pig was killed on sight. Every child under fifteen found roaming the streets was marched to the stocks and scourged.

For months the town lost all its normal bustle. There was no work for craftsmen and only essential food could be bought at the market stalls. Then the sickness died out almost as suddenly as it had started, and the cleansing began. Anything infected or suspect had to be washed or burned. Dozens of thatched roofs were set on fire and scores of townspeople went off with their household goods to the Water of Leith. At no other place, "neither wells nor yet at the South Loch nor yet at the North Loch", was cleansing permitted.

In charge of the work were five professional cleansers — sturdy young men who got sixpence a day because of the danger involved. They had to stay away from other people. Even for their morning mass they could no longer go to the Kirk of St Giles but used the old people's home in St Mary's Wynd instead. To make them easily recognised, they carried a white stick with a hoop of white iron at one end.

In Leith the epidemic lasted longer. For a year and a half the port was never free of it. But luckily the export trade was not too badly affected. The Edinburgh carters went as far as Leith Hill, beside the Abbey, and from there the carters of Leith provided a service to the quayside. What the foreigners didn't know did them no harm.

While Edinburgh was recovering from the plague, James IV had time to think of a house fit for a king. The castle was an uncomfortable place, so in 1501 he

found another home for the canons of Holyrood Abbey and began to build a palace for himself beside the Abbey. Only in peacetime would anyone have chosen such a site, outside the town and quite unprotected. But the water in the wells there was excellent and the Canongate was a delightful little village ready-made for his courtiers. The palace he planned, with its lofty turrets and its lively Gallic air, bore little resemblance to the present one.

After two years the work was still far from finished. By that time he had arranged to be married in August to the youthful Princess Margaret Tudor, daughter of Henry VII of England. So the part which was finished was hastily furnished to serve as his principal residence. No expense was spared. The hangings of red and purple velvet for the Queen's bedchamber and the canopy and curtains for her bed of state cost almost £800. His own wardrobe was even more expensive. Two gowns of cloth of gold, lined with fur, cost £600 each and he had eleven pages scarcely less resplendent in velvet and cloth of gold. Even his master chef wore a velvet gown that was lined with fur. A new saddle-cloth for the King's horse cost a further £63.

James IV, like his courtiers, had expensive tastes. He was never able to keep money long in his strong boxes. But now, when he saw them emptying so fast, even he was slightly alarmed. In the early spring, with the costs still soaring, he took steps to improve his finances. He installed an alchemist in Stirling Castle and gave him five pounds of quicksilver, with "ane pair of gret bellyis". The alchemist worked hard with his furnace and bellows. He "mixed and heated the quicksilver, litharge, borax and aquavitae which the King had brought him". But day after day he searched in vain for any trace of gold in his crucible.

Meantime the wedding day drew near. Two palfreys, a litter, a coach and a long retinue accompanied the unhappy bride-to-be on her journey north through England. All along the route, great lords

came out in rich apparel to pay their respects. At Lamberton the Scottish nobility was waiting — five hundred of them on horseback — and at Dalkeith for the first time she met her royal bridegroom. That day many of her attendants were mightily impressed by the King's horsemanship but she was more enchanted by his musical gifts. He played the clavichord and the lute with such a delicate air that it gave her "grett plaisur to here hym". Until then the very thought of marriage had left her slightly petrified, for she was scarcely fourteen and looked much younger.

She stayed four days at Dalkeith and then, in a rich gown of cloth of gold, she rode in the litter with the King at her side on the last few miles of her journey to Edinburgh. On the outskirts they paused for a moment to kiss the holy relics that some Grey Friars and Black Friars had brought. At the Netherbow Port they stopped again, to kiss the armbone of St Giles. Crowds thronged the route. Lords and ladies and gentlefolk watched from the houses along the street. There was free wine for all, in a fountain beside the market cross. And next day, in the abbey church, the little princess became Queen of Scotland.

A year later Edinburgh was again in the grip of the plague. At the far end of the Burgh Muir, in a lonely spot at the foot of Blackford Hill, huts were erected and some medical aid provided. Beside the huts a chapel was built and dedicated to St Roque, the patron saint of the afflicted. Round about there was plenty of room for burial pits.

Meantime the search for the source of the infection went on. Rotting garbage fell under suspicion. Until then, Thomas Glendinning, the bellman, had done all the scavenging unaided. Now he got two able-bodied assistants, as well as a horse, a covered cart and all the equipment he needed. From the Castle Hill right down to the head of Leith Walk the filth and fulzie were cleared away. But it was not easy in the closes, especially if they had only earthen paths. Cobbles were much

easier. A long-term project had already begun to lay these in all the closes at the rate of forty roods per annum. But that took time. Edinburgh, with its lack of rivers, was a difficult town to keep clean. Diverting the Water of Leith might have been one way, suggested a writer in 1521, but even he admitted it would be costly.

As the plague raged on, fumes of burning tallow became suspect. So the half-dozen candle-makers in the town were forbidden to work where there was any risk of polluting the High Street air. Furriers and skinners too were no longer allowed to shake their fleeces or skins in the street, for the dust might be dangerous. But it was generally felt that the fishmarket and the flesh-market were more likely sources of infection. New rules were made for the flesh-market. The stands had to be covered with clean canvas and the meat with clean linen, and the salesmen had to see that their aprons were clean too. Shoppers were no less fastidious then than they are today. To avoid upsetting their feelings, the display of nolts' heads and entrails was banned. These had to be sold only "quietly in private places".

At the fishmarket more drastic action was taken. In 1508 it was moved out of the built-up area, down the hill to the hollow beside the North Loch. The provost and his eight chaplains in the Church of the Holy Trinity can hardly have liked that, for the new site was just on the other side of their dyke. And fish merchants, as everyone knew, were not always ideal neighbours. When the bailies went there on tours of inspection, a sergeant or two always went with them to see that they were not "destitute in time of need". It was, in fact, a change which pleased no one. Eventually the market was moved back into the town.

\*     \*     \*

Perhaps it was the recurring outbreaks of plague which gave the King his absorbing and very practical interest in medical science. He could apply leeches with all the skill of a professional.

*In Greyfriars Churchyard, Death still haunts the grave of*
*James Borthwick of Stow, the Edinburgh surgeon apothecary.*

Whether he was an equally good dentist is not altogether certain. But one of his servants got 14s "because the King pullit furth his teeth" and the royal barber-surgeon got the same amount when two of his were removed. It was not a vast sum when you consider that another palace servant got 28s for a single session with the leeches.

It was in the reign of James IV, in the year 1505, that the surgeons of Edinburgh drew up the rules of their craft and the city's Royal College of Surgeons began its long history. For many years the craft included barbers but this does not mean that barbers ever performed operations. It was like the hammermen with their blacksmiths and silversmiths. No one expected a blacksmith to make treasures in silver and gold, or took his horse to a silversmith when it cast a shoe. In the same way, only those who had served a long apprenticeship under a master surgeon could hope to become surgeons themselves.

Theirs was the first company of crafts, the most honoured of all, and even in their traditions they had a natural dignity. Each year, when they received the body of an executed criminal for dissection, they gathered at their altar in the church and offered a prayer for the dead man's soul. Their rules were drafted by a perfectionist. "Every man," declared one of these, "aucht to knaw the nature and substance of every thing that he werkis, or ellis he is negligent." There was an air of friendliness, too, within the craft. It was the only one where an apprentice, having passed his final examination and been enrolled as a member, was expected to invite all his fellow-craftsmen to dinner. Except for the goldsmiths, they were the only craft drawn almost entirely from the merchant class. And they had one quite unique privilege. Though any Edinburgh merchant could import wines and spirits, and any innkeeper could sell them, only members of the barber craft could make or sell whisky. It was not that the surgeons liked it specially. They would have thought it a poor substitute for claret. But for their patients it was the nearest thing they had to an anaesthetic.

Those surgeons of Edinburgh, by all accounts, achieved some remarkable cures. One of them, Robert Henderson, got a grant of twenty merks from the Town Council for his astonishing work. The citation said he replaced the hands of a man who had them severed in an accident; he saved the lives of two people who had been run through the body by French swordsmen; and he brought a woman out alive after two days in the grave.

But the sick in those days did not rely only on surgeons and healing wells and holy relics. They had their medicines too, their herbal remedies. Half-a-century earlier, when booths were first being put into the Bellhouse, one of these became an apothecary's shop. It remained so until the reign of James IV, and then there was a move to use the premises as a money-lending business for merchants, there being no banks in those days. When the King heard of it, he wrote to the Council urging them to insist that the booth should be let to another apothecary instead. He even offered to provide a suitable tenant. It had been an apothecary's booth in his grandsire's time, he pointed out, and the need still existed.

By then, another of the King's dreams was turning into reality. With the encouragement of Bishop Elphinstone of Aberdeen, he took Scotland out of the age of scribes and manuscripts into the age of printing. The bishop disliked the English service book. He wanted one "eftir our awin Scottis use, and with legendis of Scottis sancts". So, in 1507, the King gave Walter Chepman and Andrew Myllar, two burgesses of Edinburgh, a licence to "bring hame ane prent [printing house] with al stuf belangand tharto and expert men to use the samyn".

Though printing in England began thirty years earlier, the atmosphere in Chepman & Myllar's workshop was much more Continental than English. Myllar is said to have learned the craft

in Rouen and to have brought at least some of his type from there. Very quickly the firm established its reputation with a magnificent edition of Bishop Elphinstone's Breviary in two volumes.

The King and Queen often visited this printing-house in the Cowgate, at the foot of Blackfriars Wynd, and there King James used to try his prentice hand at typesetting. Another regular visitor was William Dunbar, that most delightful of sour-faced poets, who gained the patronage of the King to become Scotland's first professional man of letters. Several of Dunbar's poems were printed there.

The hangers-on at Court inspired one of Dunbar's satires. In another, he described the Edinburgh he would have liked to see — a city where gold and silk were on sale at the market cross, and merchants and innkeepers never overcharged. But the Edinburgh of his day was not like that. No gold or silk, only curds and milk, were sold at the market cross, and cockles and wilks and tripe at the Tron. Along the gloomy Stinking Style, between the church and the Luckenbooths, the merchants were as jammed as in a honeycomb. And the main street—that fairest of streets—was defiled by the stench of haddock and skate, while tailors and soutars and other such common folk lowered the whole tone of the place. The beggars were worst of all —

Your burgh of beggaris is ane nest . . .
All honest folk they do molest,
    Sa piteouslie they cry and rame;
    Think ye nocht shame?

And certainly there was a host of beggars, not only in Dunbar's time but for many years after.

He drew a much more enticing picture in another poem, when he was trying to persuade the King to return from Stirling, where he had gone to avoid the plague. The merry town of Edinburgh, he assured the King, was a far better place than the Hell of the Grey Friars monastery in Stirling and at Holyroodhouse the food was sublime —

Ye may in Hevin here with us dwell,
To eat swan, cran, partrik and plover
And every fish that swimis in river,
To drink with us the new fresh wine
That grew upon the river of Rhine,
Fresh fragrant clarets out of France,
Of Angiers and of Orleans,
With mony ane course of great daintie;
Say ye Amen, for charitie . . .

Come hame and dwell no moir in Stirling;
From hideous Hell come hame and dwell.

Life in Edinburgh, in fact, could be rather pleasant, especially when the plague stayed away. One of the happiest days of the year was the first Sunday in May, when the townspeople marched out to the Burgh Muir to bring home the summer. The Abbot of Unreason presided over that grand ceremony and, though he had never taken holy orders, he was always a man of substance as well as fun. There were times, indeed, when he seemed to be chosen for the substance alone. The Provost of Edinburgh made the choice and one nominee declined the office because he felt he was quite unsuitable. He explained that he "joked wi' deeficulty" and was far more accustomed to higher and graver matters. Francis Bothwell made a similar excuse when he was chosen for the lesser role of Little John. By then it was beginning to change from an Abbot of Unreason to a Robin Hood procession. But there was little difference between the two.

Each year they marched down the High Street with drums beating, banners flying and cannons roaring. There were garlanded horsemen, as well as guisers, dancers and a little boy bishop surrounded by "deevilots". The crafts with their banners were there and in pride of place, just in front of the Abbot himself, the wealthy Hammermen marched in full armour with their drums and banners. One group of them represented King Herod and six of his knights, with two of his learned doctors.

After spending the day on the Burgh Muir, they all paraded back in the evening, carrying birch branches as their forefathers had done since time

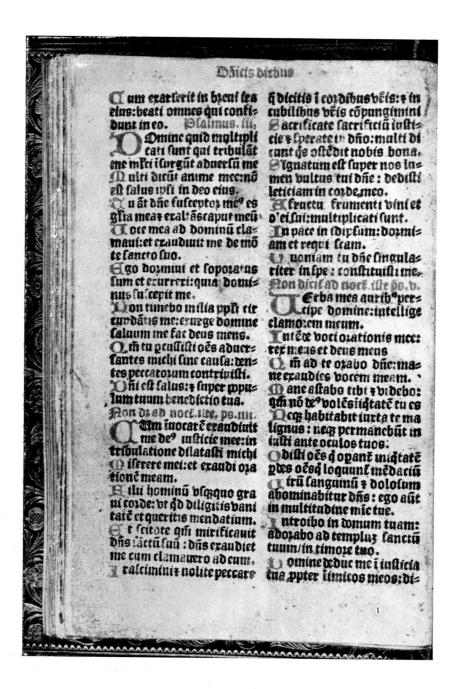

*Bishop Elphinstone's Breviary —*

[54]

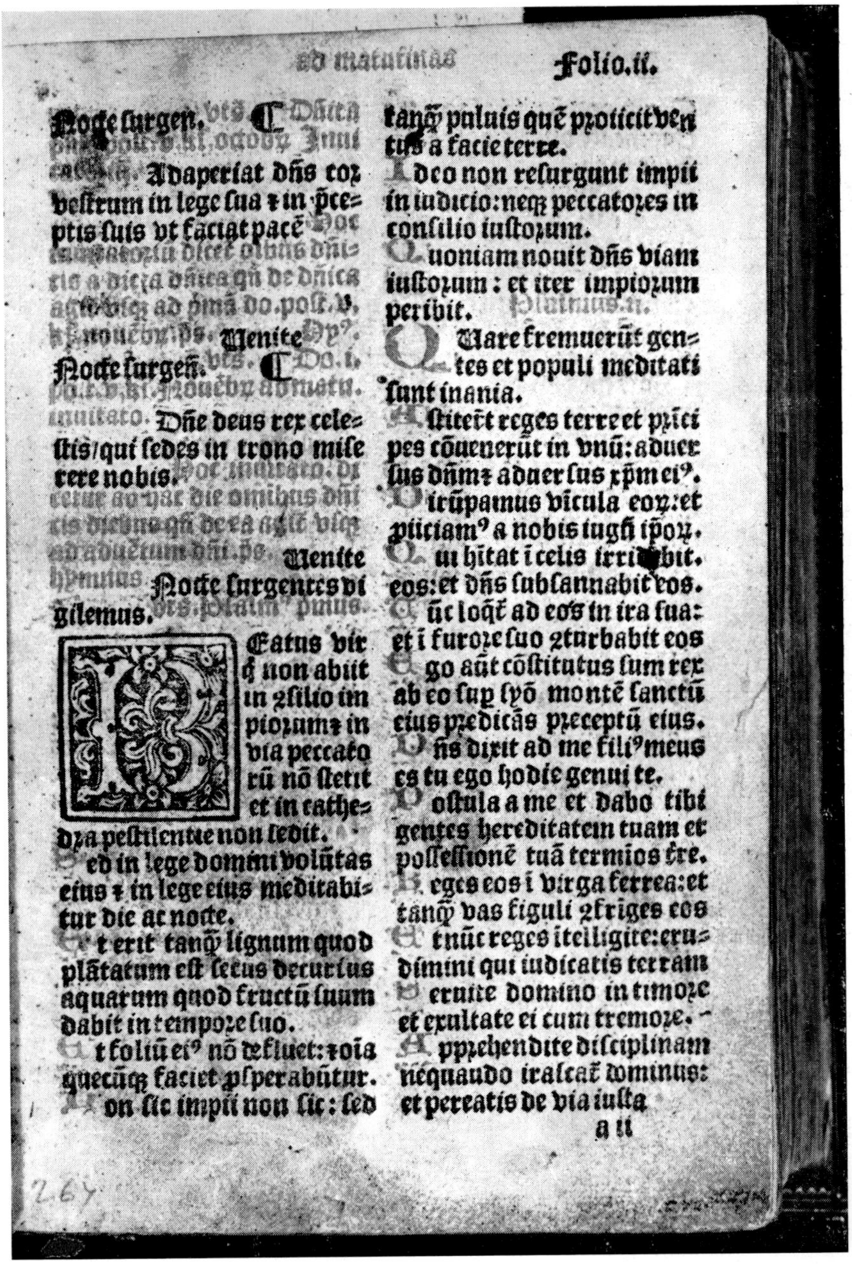

Nocte surgen. ꝯ C Dicta
caꝑ. Adaperiat dñs cor
vestrum in lege sua ⁊ in ꝑce-
ptis suis vt faciat pacē Doc
... dicet obñs dñi
cis a dicta dñica ꝗ de dñica
agit ⁊ñꝗ; ad ꝫmā do.post.v.
... Venite
Nocte surgen. C Do. i.
... Monebꝛ a dñicu
mutato. Dñe deus rex cele-
stis/qui sedēs in trono mise
rere nobis.
... Venite
hꝑmnus Nocte surgentes vi
gilemus.

Eatus vir
ꝗ non abiit
in ꜿsilio im
pioꝛum⁊ in
via peccato
rū nō stetit
et in cathe-
dꝛa pestilentie non sedit.
ed in lege domini volūtas
eius ⁊ in lege eius meditabi-
tur die ac nocte.
t erit tanꝗ lignum quod
plātatum est secus decurlus
aquarum quod fructū suum
dabit in tempoꝛe suo.
t foliū ei⁹ nō defluet:⁊ oīa
quecūꝗ; faciet ꝑsperabūtur.
on sic impii non sic: sed

**Right column:**

tanꝗ puluis quē proiicit vē
tus a facie terre.
deo non resurgunt impii
in iudicio:neꝗ; peccatoꝛes in
consilio iustoꝛum.
uoniam nouit dñs viam
iustoꝛum : et iter impioꝛum
peribit.
Uare fremuerūt gen-
tes et populi meditati
sunt inania.
stiterūt reges terre et princi
pes cōuenerūt in vnū:aduer
sus dūm⁊ aduerlus ꝛꝓm ei⁹.
irūpamus vicula eoꝛ:et
proiiciam⁹ a nobis iugū ipoꝛ.
ui hitat i celis irridebit
eos:et dñs subsannabit eos.
ūc loꝗ̄ ad eos in ira sua:
et i furoꝛe suo ꜿturbabit eos
go aūt cōstitutus sum rex
ab eo sup syō montē sanctū
eius predicās preceptū eius.
ñs dixit ad me fili⁹ meus
es tu ego hodie genui te.
ostula a me et dabo tibi
gentes hereditatem tuam et
possessionē tuā termios ꝭe.
eges eos i virga ferrea:et
tanꝗ vas figuli ꜿfriges eos
tnūc reges iteiligite:eru
dimini qui iudicatis terram
eruite domino in timoꝛe
et exultate ei cum tremoꝛe.
pprehendite disciplinam
nequando irascat dominus:
et pereatis de via iusta
a ii

one of the earliest examples of printing in Scotland.

[55]

immemorial, when they brought home summer to the town.

It was not only in May that Edinburgh saw the Abbot of Unreason. In the new-built Holyroodhouse he appeared at Christmas too. The celebrations began on 6th December, St Nicholas Day, when the boy bishop and his deevilots, all abbey choristers, burst into the royal apartments and roared out parodies of the psalms they so solemnly chanted during the rest of the year. After they had withdrawn, well rewarded, the Abbot of Unreason arrived to preside over the lustier second stage. But it was not the same abbot who brought summer home in May. At the King's yule a humble member of the palace staff was usually chosen for the role.

James IV had many interests but his special delight was jousting, that most elegant of kingly sports. Gone were the crude old days, when no tournament was complete without a rich spattering of bloodstains. The jousting was no longer meant to hurt. The spectacle was what mattered. And James IV had an uncanny flair for staging displays which won renown all over civilised Europe.

The royal tilting ground, known as the Barreres or Barres, was down below the castle where King's Stables Road now enters the Grassmarket. The name of the road is as old as the tournaments themselves, for it was in those stables of James IV, just west of this "Place of the Spear Sports", that the champions' horses and attendants were housed.

Up in the castle the ladies of the Court watched from richly decorated stands that hung over the castle ramparts. It was a colourful scene below, with banners everywhere, sumptuous pavilions and lavish drapings. The air was full of the thunder of horses' hooves interspersed with the music of fiddlers and harpers. And, after the pageantry and the feats of martial skill, the thrills of the day were rounded off with nights of feasting in the castle, in the great hall that had been built only a few years before.

Oddly enough, James IV never really understood how important it was for people to have class distinctions and colour bars. There was, you might almost say, an international lack of understanding about that. Two Moorish girls spent three years at the Court of King James as attendants on his favourite daughter. Soon after their arrival, he gave them presents of identical dresses in green kersey, with kirtles in red of the same material, and collars and hoods of Holland cloth. At 43s 2d each, those dresses were not extravagantly expensive. One in black and tan for another attendant, Marjory Lindsay, cost 77s with all the trimmings. But still they were dear enough, when you remember that for less than that the King could have bought a dozen felt hats for himself. These cost him only 3s 6d each.

The two Moorish girls were not the only foreign ones who moved in Court circles. A pretty negress presided as Queen of Beauty at a Black Lady Tournament in 1507 and she was such an outstanding success that the following year he had to hold a similar tournament on a still grander scale. The great Lord of Aubigny brought a party of friends from France for the second one. It was the most lavish of all the tournaments. Even the entry forms for overseas competitors were sumptuously lettered and illuminated in gold.

Round the tilting ground were five pavilions, the largest in silk with standards flying above. Two of the others were in taffeta and two in canvas. For their fringes alone, almost two hundred yards of silk were needed. There were winged beasts too, prominent among the decorations. But everything was on a lavish scale at this second "Tournament of the Wild Knight and the Black Lady".

The royal needlewomen were busy beforehand, embroidering flowers and "panises" on yard after yard of taffeta that had been specially bought in Flanders. That was used to drape the chair triumphal, in which the Black Lady rode in state. There were over 170 yards of the taffeta in five different colours.

The cloth of gold for her damask gown came from London and, at almost £5 a yard, the material for that cost over £30. Two girls and two squires attended her, the girls in gowns of Flemish taffeta and the squires in white damask. The challengers also wore white.

But the cynosure of every eye was the Wild Knight, the champion of the Queen of Beauty. Surrounded by his wild men in goatskins, with harts' horns on their heads, he had two squires as well, in cloth of gold doublets. In spite of his swarthy face and comic antics, the Wild Knight was easily recognised by his shoulder-length hair as the King himself.

Four years later other two black ladies, with an Irish one and several Scottish, were ladies of the Queen's chamber. On New Year's Day the Queen gave each of them a ring made by John Aitken, the goldsmith, in his workshop at Stirling Castle.

\*     \*     \*

Big changes in the town were taking place at that time. In Scotland as a whole there was a famine of wood. One traveller commented that "had Christ been betrayed in this country . . . Judas had sooner found the grace of repentance than a tree to hang himself on". Parliament seemed to hold the same opinion, at its meeting in Edinburgh in 1504. "The wod of Scotland," it recorded, "is utterlie distroyit." Yet only seven years later there was such a glut in the Edinburgh district that the Town Council was trying desperately to get rid of it.

Beer was partly the cause of the glut. When the surplus crops of the Lothians were turned into malt or beer, they could be highly profitable. So in 1510 the Town Council began to feu sites on the Burgh Muir for all who wanted to build a malt kiln, a coble or barn, for the business of malt-making. The Provost of Edinburgh took advantage of the offer. Bailie Walter Young feued another of the three-acre sites. The laird of Haltoun took yet another.

In making the ground ready, the feuars cut down so many large trees that they were unable to get rid of them all. So in 1511 the Town Council decided that any burgess of Edinburgh who bought enough of this wood to make a new front for his house would be allowed to extend the house seven feet into the street. There was a rush to do so. And thus the width of the Royal Mile was reduced by fourteen feet.

Only one of those houses, "John Knox's House", still has a wooden frontage; and behind the frontage is a stone-built house. But there were still many similar ones when William Maitland wrote his history of Edinburgh, fully two centuries ago. According to him, they were all stone-built. "The buildings which before had stonern fronts," he wrote, "were now converted into wood and the burgh into a wooden city."

There was an obvious advantage in having a frontage of wood. Glass-making had not yet begun in Scotland and not even the King had permanent window panes in his palaces. When he moved around his kingdom, the tapestries, beds and windows were sent on ahead from one palace to another. And so, for most of the year, those royal palaces were unfurnished and the windows gaped uninvitingly. It was scarcely surprising, then, that glass was beyond the reach of the householders of Edinburgh. They made little round holes in the wooden fronts and stuck their heads through to watch the passing scene.

While those dull frontages were going up all along the Royal Mile, something much more exciting was happening in and around Edinburgh. Up in the castle Britain's first armaments factory had gone into production. Under the guidance of French experts, its forges were turning out brass cannons all day long, and into the night by candlelight. On the shore west of Leith a royal dockyard had been established too, with a huddle of houses that were already becoming known as Newhaven. There a ship was being built that by all the standards of those days was colossal. When Columbus discovered America a few years earlier, his three

*The Hare Stone.*

house had to display a white cloth, nailed in a prominent place on the stairs or door.

By the middle of June the disease was rampant in the Dean Village and no one from there was allowed into Edinburgh. But not even the plague could put a stop to the work at the castle. At Newhaven too the ship repairers were as pressed as ever. Three of the King's ships were having their hulls cleaned and tallowed. The damaged hull of another was being repaired. And the Great Michael was being fitted with a new set of masts. Just when the pest in Dean Village was confirmed, a convoy of fifty carts set off from the castle for Leith, every cart laden with guns. Even in England it was common knowledge by then that daily consignments of arms and artillery were being shipped to Leith from Campvere in the Low Countries.

If there were any lingering doubts about what the King was planning, they vanished in July 1513, when he sent out a summons to war. The men of Edinburgh, headed by the Provost and bailies, went off with their banners and standards, hurriedly fashioned at the castle during the previous few weeks. The craftsmen had their Blue Blanket. But the King's royal banner in crimson and gold was not there. Because its fringes were still unfinished, it had to be sent by special messenger after the army had gone.

A stone on a pedestal in front of Morningside Parish Church has an inscription which tells us that this was the Bore-Stone where the royal standard was unfurled that day, when the men of Edinburgh mustered on the Burgh Muir in readiness for war. But there was, of course, no royal banner to unfurl. In fact, the Edinburgh contingent did not muster there at all but at Ellam in the Lammermuirs.

There is no doubt, however, that the stone is a relic of far-off days. When the Kings of Scotland went hunting on the Burgh Muir, from the thirteenth century on, the Laird of Penicuik was duty-bound to come to this stone and give three

ships had a total crew of 88. This Scottish warship, the Great Michael, was to have a complement of 307, with six score gunners in addition. She was eighty yards long and, though most of her timbers were brought from Norway, the only woodlands left in Fife when she was launched in 1512 were the royal woods at Falkland Palace. The Great Michael was one of the largest ships in Europe, with none to equal her in England or France.

The plague had broken out again by that time and a suspicion was growing that those who recovered became carriers of the disease. So a new hazard arose for those who turned sick. Even if they recovered they were still doomed to die if in the next forty days they dared to speak to any healthy person. During that time they had to carry a white stick or wear a white cloth sewn on the breast. Even the

blasts on his horn. Not to have done so would have meant the forfeiture of his barony. But in those days the stone stood a short distance away from its present site and it was the Hare Stone, not the Bore-Stone.

\* \* \*

Some ten days after the muster, the royal army was close to the English Border and the plague was spreading fast through Edinburgh. For a fortnight, all sales at the market were banned except for meat and drink. Business in the Luckenbooths and the Krames came to a standstill too. There the shutters remained "steikit and clossit, and thair durris nocht opinit".

While the townspeople walked in dread of the plague, scarcely less alarming was the number of army deserters who came pouring in. Thirteen householders, whose back dykes were broken down, were ordered to have them repaired at once to keep the intruders out.

On 10th September, just when a Council meeting was about to begin, a rumour began to spread like wildfire through the town that the King was dead and the army overwhelmed in battle. It was too persistent to ignore. That night the Council issued their first emergency regulations:

"Forsamekill as thair is ane greit rumour now laitlie rysen within this toun tuiching our Souerane Lord and his army,

THE KING, WITH THE FLOWER OF HIS ARMY, HAD FALLEN AT FLODDEN THE PREVIOUS EVENING

of the quhilk we understand thair is cumin na veritie as yit, thairfore we charge in our said Souerane Lord the Kingis name . . . that all maner of personis, nychtbouris within the samyn, haue reddye thair fensabill geir and wapponis for weir.

"And also chargis that all wemen, and specialie vagaboundis, that thai pas to thair labouris and be nocht sene vpoun the gait clamorand and cryand . . . and that the vther wemen of gude pas to the kirk and pray quhane tyme requiris for our Souerane Lord and his armye and nychtbouris being thairat."

The full extent of the disaster was soon confirmed. The two armies had met at Branxton Hill and, as most of the Scottish officers and men were armed with spears fully fifteen feet long, as well as great swords, they put their trust in these and sent their horses to the rear. The generals insisted that the King should also stay at the rear, directing the battle. As a soldier he was worth only one man, while as a general he might be worth a hundred thousand. But he refused to fight anywhere except in the forefront, with a spear and a sword like the rest, and his crimson and gold standard flying proudly overhead.

A contemporary Italian tells us that he fought as bravely as the bravest of his followers. Five men died on his spear-point before it was shattered in his hands and he fell, pierced by an arrow and gashed by a bill on the battlefield of Flodden. The English estimated that at least ten thousand Scots died with him, and many lie buried just downhill in Branxton churchyard, in a great pit into which men and horses were thrown together, and covered with a foot-thick layer of earth.

# 6

## The Flowers of the Forest
## are a' wede away

SCOTLAND GOT another child king after Flodden, for James V was scarcely seventeen months old when his father died. Four years later he was brought to Edinburgh — not to the comfort of Holyroodhouse but to the safety of the "wyndy and richt unpleasand castell and royk of Edinburgh".

The town's Flodden Wall was taking shape by then. It was begun only seven months after the battle, when everyone with a back dyke was given a fortnight to build it up into a defence against English invaders. Taxes were imposed too, to meet the cost of strengthening the town and buying more artillery. But after a time the urgency became blunted. Even forty years later the wall was still not quite finished.

It ran from the castle across the Grassmarket and up the Vennel, where it can still be seen with its one surviving tower. Turning east from there, it followed what is now the northern boundary of Heriot's Hospital and the west and south boundaries of Greyfriars Churchyard, then along South College Street and Drummond Street to the Pleasance, where it turned north to join the Cowgate at the foot of St Mary's Street.

Even in the first year after Flodden, many a merchant would have told you that getting Edinburgh's trade back to normal was much more important than any wall. Some leading inhabitants of Leith were beginning to trade on their own, quite unlawfully. To put a stop to that, the Edinburgh merchants drew up a set of rules for their gild, just as the tradesmen had done for their crafts. So

the Kirk of St Giles got yet another altar. The new Aisle of the Holy Blood, on the south side of the church, became the merchants' aisle.

Edinburgh by then had a new chapel too, west of Causewayside at what later became known as Sciennes Road. It was a good place for a chapel. One of the most potent of all the healing wells around Edinburgh was there, on the Burgh Muir. From time immemorial, pilgrims with skin diseases had gone to this balm well to be cured. It was no ordinary water. "Oil," said one traveller in 1539, "flows out of the ground."

Services in the chapel began about six months before the battle of Flodden, with a chaplain in charge and a hermit as his assistant. There were no special rules for the chaplain, for he was its founder, John Crawford. But the hermit had to be elderly and willing to keep the place well dusted, apart from his other duties. He lived there and wore a white gown with a picture of John the Baptist on his breast. Each morning he prayed for the founder and at masses each day he said fifteen Paternosters, fifteen Ave Marias and one Credo, in front of the image of the Crucifixion.

But that lasted only four years. In 1517 the widows and kinsfolk of some of Flodden's dead were allowed to turn the hermitage into a nunnery — the Nunnery of St Catherine of Siena. Each year a small part of its revenue came from ancestors of Robert Burns at Bogjorgan and Inchbreck in the Mearns. Each day the nuns sang high mass. And by their general helpfulness, they won golden

opinions from all their neighbours.

Scarcely had they moved in when the plague, never far away, came back to Edinburgh. By the following year it was so bad that a workman was transferred from the huts on the Burgh Muir to tackle the problem of the dead. They were lying unburied in their houses. At nine o'clock each evening he began his round, and all through the night he carried off the sick to the plague huts and the dead to the burial pits. He was not allowed to break into locked rooms in the houses he visited but if he found a room unlocked he could either burn the clothes he found there or clean them for his own use. At five in the morning he finished his ghoulish task. The rest of the burying had to wait until darkness fell again.

The plague was not the only dreaded sickness in those days. More lingering and loathsome was leprosy. In Biblical times Job knew all about it. King Robert the Bruce was one of its Scottish victims. By 1520 it was gradually being mastered, though its cause was still as baffling as ever. Some said it came from eating fish, either raw or stale, and in Edinburgh people noted that an outbreak occurred just after some stale fish was given to the poor at the castle gate. But no one was sure. The only fact beyond dispute was that isolation prevented it spreading. So the lepers were housed outside the town. In 1520 a new home was built for them on what had been for years a tilting ground, in the shadow of the Calton Hill. A group of dedicated Carmelite friars looked after them.

*       *       *

The town was still growing in size and, though no one had yet begun to talk about its Royal Mile, already there was a move in that direction. People were referring to the King's Road, when they meant the Lawnmarket, the High Street or the Canongate. Even the lawyers in their official documents were doing so by 1523. In January that year the Church of St Giles got annuities from four local properties. Three were recorded in Latin as being in the King's Road (*vicus regius*), while the other was described as in "Nudry's Wynd . . . on the south side of the King's Road". About the same time, Alexander Alesse wrote a description of Edinburgh. After referring to the palace he added that "a long ridge called the King's Road extends from there right to the Maidens' Castle".

It was a well-built road, neatly paved with square-dressed stones. For many years, experts had been coming from France when any repairs were needed. In 1532 we read of two French paviours renewing the surface.

The most famous of the French experts was Marlin, who became part of the tradition of Edinburgh. There used to be six paving stones, shaped like a coffin lid, set into the roadway just opposite the Tron Church. Everyone knew that they marked the grave of this Frenchman who first paved the High Street. In honour of his achievement, the Council let him have his burial place in the middle of the street he had laid, at the upper end of the flesh-market. There was no Tron Church in his day. But after his death there was a Marlin's Wynd between Peebles Wynd and Niddry's Wynd. It ran from his grave in the High Street down to the Cowgate. In 1637 a start was made with the building of the Tron Church across its northern end but ten years later the rest of the close was still shown in a bird's-eye view of Edinburgh by Captain John Slezer. And in 1974, when restoration work was going on in the church, part of its cobbled surface was rediscovered under the floor.

The High Street roadway was not the only place where dressed stones could be seen. We have already had indications by earlier writers that stone-built houses were by no means uncommon along the street. Alesse goes much further. According to him, those houses of stone existed in large numbers not only facing the High Street but in the closes too. And he was unlikely to be wrong, for he was a native of Edinburgh.

*James Mosman's house 1647*

In his description there is not a word about wooden houses, though he does mention bricks. The city, he wrote, was "not built of bricks but of boulders and dressed stones, and so there are individual houses that might be compared with great palaces". Pointing out that the King's Road had notable houses on both sides, the more imposing of dressed stone, he added that the many closes were all adorned with excellent buildings.

One of the houses he must have known was just above Peebles Wynd. A handsome mansion, it was reputed to have been built about 1430, with statues of saints in niches all along the dressed stone frontage. The saints were smashed at the Reformation but the house survived until the late eighteenth century.

Mowbray House, farther down the street, would have been equally familiar. It too had lost its new look before he was born, though it still survives today. And next to it was where John Arres lived — another substantial house, projecting out

into the street at the foot of the wide market place.

Mr Arres was a friend of John Mosman, Scotland's leading craftsman in silver and gold, whose handiwork can still be seen in the Crown Room at Edinburgh Castle. It was he who designed the royal crown with its precious stones, its oriental pearls and its blue and red enamel, the oldest of the British crowns.

A son of John Mosman married Mariota Arres and this James Mosman eventually became the owner of the High Street house. Like his father he was a silversmith; he was master of the mint. Like his father too he disliked the Reformers. John Knox, the fiery minister of St Giles, is unlikely ever to have crossed his threshold. And so it seems slightly odd that through the centuries his house should have changed its name, until now it is always called "John Knox's House".

Down in the Canongate Alesse would have recognised at least part of Huntly

*James Mosman's house 1975*

*The Wealthy Hammerman*

House, built like a little fortress with a loophole guarding even the approach from Edinburgh through the Netherbow Gate. In his day the house had no door facing the street. A port-cochère led to a little courtyard at the back and, when the gate was shut and barred, you were safe from sudden attack. That was an important part of planning in those days.

But in the Edinburgh that Alesse knew, the most interesting district was neither the High Street nor the Canongate. It was down beside the wells, in the Cowgate. This, he reminds us, was "where the nobility and chief citizens dwell and the greatest in the land have their palaces, where nothing is cheap or mean but all things are magnificent".

Cardinal Beaton lived there. So did the Earl of Buchan. Next to the Earl was the town house of the Lady of Borthwick. And just beyond was the mansion of Sir Thomas Tod. On the south side, close to the Black Friars chapel, lived Walter Chepman the printer, whose mansion had an orchard and the luxury of its own private well. Soon a chaplain and seven bedesmen were to join the nobility. An old folk's home, with a chapel attached, was about to be built at the west end of that exclusive street. The chapel, known for centuries as the Magdalen Chapel, still survives as one of the most interesting of Edinburgh's ancient buildings.

It was Michael Macqueen the Hammerman, and his wife Janet, who brought the bedesmen. Mr Macqueen was probably a goldsmith like the Mosmans. Certainly he was a man of consequence, for he had his own heraldic arms and an ample fortune. There may actually be a statue of him above the tower doorway of the chapel — a delightful carving of a prosperous Hammerman dressed in the height of fashion.

When Mr Macqueen was old and near to death, he decided to build the bedesmen's house as an insurance into the hereafter. But he died about 1537, before he had time to start it. After his death there were difficulties in getting it begun. His share of the cost was to have been £700 and several of his friends had promised the rest. But by 1540 the Reformation was within sight and his friends lost their enthusiasm. His widow, with no prospect of help, decided to go ahead alone. She dipped into her private fortune for a further £2000 and, defying the whole trend of public opinion, built this Roman Catholic chapel and old folk's home at her own expense. It was the last Catholic chapel to be erected in Edinburgh for almost three centuries.

By 1544 the bedesmen's house and the chapel with its barrel-vaulted ceiling were finished and the bedesmen moved in. At seven in the morning their aristocratic neighbours rubbed the sleep from their eyes to the rhythmic toll of the chapel bell. Then the voices of the bedesmen could be heard, murmuring the Lord's Prayer five times and the Angelical Salutation fifty. Just after dinner, they went down on their knees with their chaplain in front of the great altar for another prayer cycle which included five Pater Nosters, fifty Ave Marias and a Creed.

Their chaplain had to be a man of

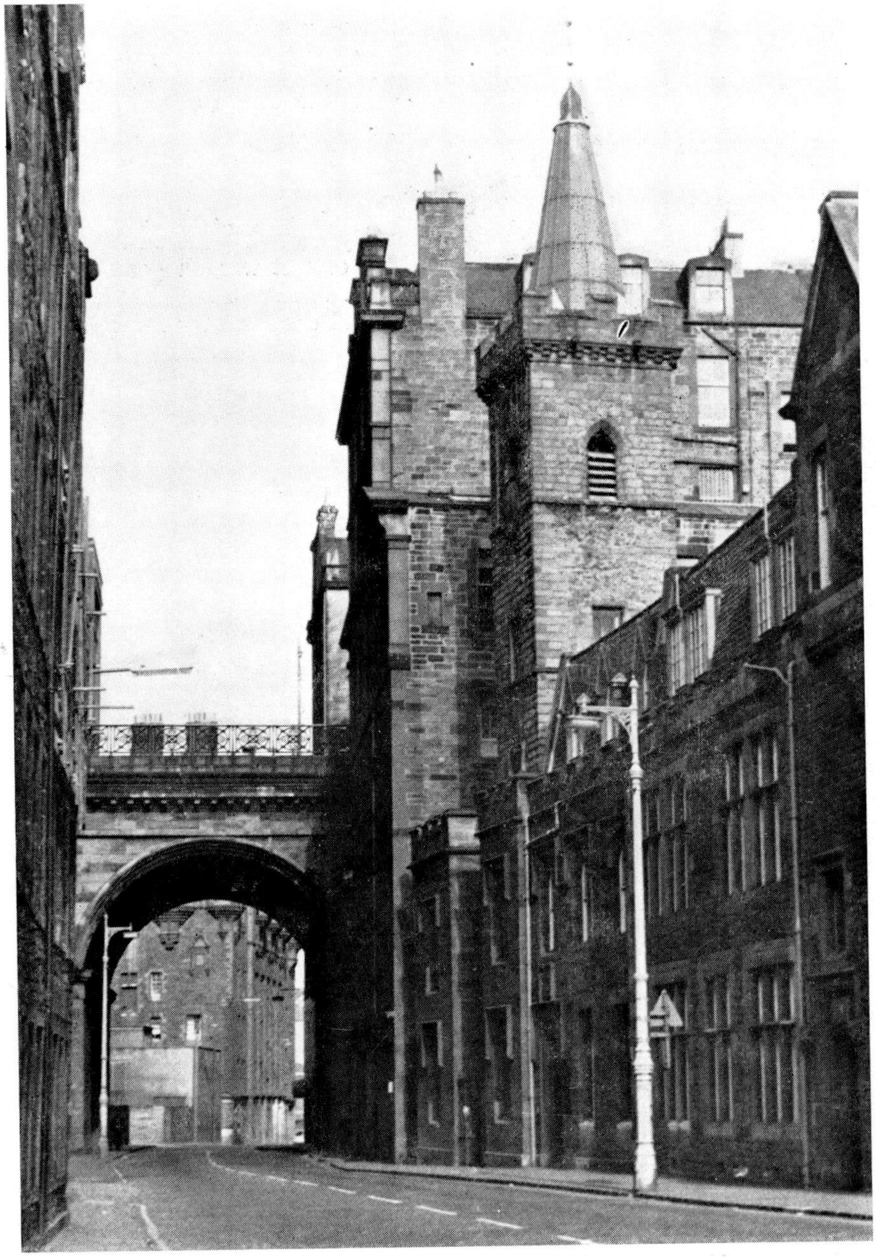

*The Magdalen Chapel.*

*The Magdalen Chapel soon after the tower was added in 1625.*

to enjoy a good life with all the trimmings, the church was the life for you. That applied not only to humble chaplains in charge of bedesmen's houses but to abbots, priors and bishops as well. People were broad-minded about small misdemeanours, as was only right in a permissive society. So when Sir David Lindsay wrote a satire on the churchmen of his day, it was all good fun and no offence. Even the King went to see his play and chuckle over the confessions of one of its characters, a worthy Abbot —

ABBOT

There is na monks from Carrick to Carraill,
That fairs better and drinks mair helsum aill.
My prior is ane man of great devotion:
Thairfor, daylie, he gets ane double portion.

SCRYBE

My Lord, how have ye keipt your thrie vows?

ABBOT

. . . My paramours is baith als fat and fair
As ony wench intill the toun of Air.
I send my sons to Pareis, to the scuillis,
I traist in God that thay sall be no fuillis,
And all my douchters I have weill provydit;
Now judge ye, gif my office be weill gydit.

In 1542 James V sent an army into England to disaster at Solway Moss and a few days later he died. His heir, the infant Mary Queen of Scots, was only one week old.

Mary of Guise had little time to mourn the dead King. She now had a marriageable daughter. Henry VIII of England could see a Union of the Crowns by the marriage of the infant to his son Prince Edward, and when the Scots rudely turned down his advances, he roughened up the wooing. In 1544 he sent an army north to destroy Edinburgh, so that the Scots would have forever "a perpetuel memory of the vengeaunce of God . . . for their faulschode and disloyailtye". You could hardly blame him for being annoyed. His ambassador had just told him that the Scots hated the English — that they actually preferred the French.

In early May the Earl of Hertford reached Edinburgh with his army. Unable to storm the castle, he set fire to the

integrity, though minor indiscretions were forgiven. If he ate too well or got too drunk, quarrelled overmuch or thoughtlessly slipped into adultery or incest, he was given only three chances to mend his ways. If by the end of the year he had not improved, out he went. The bedesmen were governed by a stricter code. The only woman in their lives was the one who came each day to collect their sewage.

Though life was placid in the Cowgate, in some other parts of Edinburgh there was harsher justice. In the year when Michael Macqueen died, so did a witch on the Castle Hill, the lovely mother of the 7th Lord Glamis. Very few people thought she was a witch but everyone knew that James V disliked her and her Douglas kinsmen. Two years later, in Holyrood Abbey, he married Mary of Guise, one of the gentlest of Scotland's Queens. And that same week, on the Castle Hill, five heretics were burned.

A certain worldliness had edged its way into religion by then. If you wanted

*Holyroodhouse, drawn in 1544, when Hertford's army was still in occupation. The damage is clearly visible. In the foreground a column of English soldiers is about to enter the Canongate through the Water Gate.*

[67]

*The ruins of Edinburgh after Hertford's raid. Although there are many damaged roofs, the house walls seem to have escaped undamaged. At the foot of the High Street is the medieval Netherbow Port, replaced in 1606. Farther up is St Giles', with the Church of St Mary-in-the-Field beyond the Cowgate.*

*Lea the Victor's church at St Albans*

palace and Holyrood Abbey. In the pillage which followed, an army commander, Sir Richard Lea, carried off the brass font from the abbey and gifted it to his home church at St Albans in Hertfordshire. And just in case anyone thought it too splendid a font for the plebs in this Church of St Albans, at his own expense he had an inscription engraved on it in elegant Latin: "When Leith, a not uncelebrated town in Scotland, and Edinburgh, the principal city of them all, were on fire and burning furiously, Sir Richard Lea snatched me from the flames and took me to England. In gratitude for his generosity, I, who have hitherto been used only at the christening of the children of Kings, do now willingly perform the same task for anyone within the boundaries of England. This was the wish of Lea the victor. Farewell. A.D. 1543 and in the 36th year of Henry VIII."

For a century the font continued its democratic work and then, during the English Civil War, it was stolen again. This time it finally disappeared.

Holyroodhouse and the abbey were not the only buildings set ablaze by Hertford during his raid. Castles and towns, villages and hamlets went up in flames for miles around. At Winton, in Pencaitland parish, he destroyed the great house of Seton, built scarcely fifty years before, and its famous garden where the flower plots were surrounded by a hundred little wooden temples, with gilded bells on top. In Leith every stick of the pier and every house was burned to the ground. He found it a good town for pillaging, "more full of ryches than we thought to have founde any Scottishe toune to have been".

But Edinburgh suffered most. It was set on fire in so many places that the pungent fumes drove the soldiers out before nightfall. Next day they came back to continue the burning and it took them three days to complete. Thatched roofs and wooden frontages, with their peepholes, vanished in their hundreds in the flames. But not everything was destroyed. Though the damage was immense, after three days of burning much of the heart of Edinburgh emerged miraculously from its wooden casing to reveal a stone-built town. The burgesses didn't like what they saw. The timber fronts were replaced.

One of Hertford's men drew a picture map of the town immediately after the

raid, with the damage only too apparent. But his drawing confirms the fact that behind the wooden fronts were stone-built houses. He shows the walls still standing, though many of the roofs are badly damaged. The Canongate seems to have suffered most. It seems too, from his drawing, that already the houses of Edinburgh were being built taller than those in the Canongate, a feature which was to become increasingly marked as time went on.

\* \* \*

During the next four years, even the shortest journey out from Edinburgh was full of hazards. A strong armed escort was needed, even for a visit to Leith with a cargo for export. Day and night, companies of English horsemen thundered across the countryside and up to the very gates of the city, to pounce on the unwary and impress on everyone that the English were the master race. There were only about five hundred of those horsemen but they terrorised the inhabitants, until at long last some French troops came and drove them away.

Partly because of those horsemen and partly because nobles at home were plotting, Mary of Guise was parted from a child of her own for the second time in her life. When she married James V she had to give up the three-year-old son of her first marriage. Now the five-year-old daughter of her second marriage, Mary Queen of Scots, was smuggled off to France to avoid English capture and Scottish intrigue. There she spent the rest of her childhood sharing the royal nurseries with the Dauphin of France.

There had been changes in the Magdalen Chapel by then. Only a few weeks after the bedesmen moved in, it was damaged in Hertford's raid. Then in 1553 Mrs Macqueen died and was buried in the chapel, under a table-tomb in the south-east corner. Though a platform now covers the tomb, a hinged flap can be raised to reveal the top of the stone.

Soon after her death a new window was inserted — a very handsome one for a bedesmen's chapel. Ordinary glass was then dear and scarce but this was infinitely dearer, for it was in stained glass. It consisted of four roundels. While the lower two displayed the arms of Mr and Mrs Macqueen, the upper two bore the Royal Arms of Scotland, encircled by a thistle wreath, and the arms of Mary of Guise as Queen Regent, with a laurel wreath and a crown above. Four centuries later people still visit the chapel specially to see this window. With the passing years it has grown in value, for today it is by far the best surviving example of ancient stained glass in Scotland.

\* \* \*

There was never any shortage of food in those days, with the fertile Lothians all around. One traveller, Nicander Nucius, commented in 1545 on the wonderful multitude of oxen and sheep. "Generally also they abound in butter and cheese and milk," he added. Estienne Perlin made a similar comment six years later. Provisions in Edinburgh seemed to him as plentiful and cheap as anywhere in the world. The townspeople then were still very largely vegetarian.

Going to the market, in earlier times, had always been a pleasant experience. But now that religious differences were arising, people seemed more violent than before. There were so many disturbances at the markets that in 1552 the civic fathers had to tighten the safety regulations. As soon as the alarm bell rang or a disturbance began, all the merchants and craftsmen had to sally forth from their booths with their hand-axes, Jedburgh staves, javelins and similar long weapons. This, the Council explained, was because of the great slaughters and feuds that had already occurred and the prospect of more ahead.

That the magistrates needed the help of the burgesses was obvious enough. There was trouble everywhere — not just in the market place. One May day in 1557 the Provost himself was almost assassinated. A master tailor armed with a dagger broke into his house, inflicted

three stab wounds on a servant who intervened, and stabbed the Provost deep in the shoulder.

Six weeks later this Nicolas Rynd was brought bare-headed, barefoot and in his underclothes to the market cross. Watched by crowds of onlookers he went down on his knees before the Provost, bailies and Council, and humbly begged their forgiveness and the pardon of God. Then he was formally deprived of his civic rights and banished for ever under pain of death.

It was at night, however, that most of the crimes were committed. To combat the growing lawlessness, the street lights went on in Edinburgh. No one was allowed to be out after dark without a lantern, a torch or candle, and at five o'clock in the evening, all through the winter months, the inhabitants had to hang lanterns up in the streets and closes beside their houses. At nine o'clock the lanterns were taken down again, for everyone was expected to be indoors by then.

Still the violence continued. To any good Protestant the Kirk of St Giles was like a festering sore with its provost and prebendaries, its choristers and chaplains, candles and relics, altars and graven images. You were selling your soul to the Devil if you believed like your forefathers in such Papist delusions. In 1557, the year when the Provost of Edinburgh was stabbed, the townspeople began to cut out this canker in their bosoms.

The arm-bone of St Giles in its jewelled reliquary soon vanished, never to return. The great statue of St Giles, the one that was carried through the town each year in the St Giles Day Procession, was less easy. That statue was part of the tradition of Edinburgh — it was even on the burgh arms—and there were ugly scenes before the good folk managed to drag it out of the church and down to the North Loch, where they hurled it into the water. Later they fished it out and burned it.

That happened just before the annual procession was due to take place. The thought of cancelling the procession never entered the head of the provost of St Giles'. Borrowing another statue from the Grey Friars, he set about organising the biggest one in living memory. From all over the town he summoned layfolk and clergy to witness their faith — not soberly and prayerfully but with joyful drums and trumpets, banners and bagpipes. He even persuaded the Queen Regent to head the procession, with the statue close behind her.

Luckily she left before the end. So, with no disrespect to monarchy, the Reformers were able in the latter stages to charge in and drive the panic-stricken Catholics to flight. When peace returned to the High Street, the borrowed statue was lying in a thousand fragments on the causeway. It was the last time that a St Giles Day Procession was held in Edinburgh.

Two years later the Reformation was fast gathering momentum. An Army of the Covenant marched on Edinburgh from Perth and, with three of the city's gates in ruins, the Catholic authorities had no power to stop it. Some of the leading burgesses took home the vestments and altar vessels from St Giles' and hid them in their own homes. Many documents from the town's charter chest were hidden there too. But preparations to fight to the death were not entirely abandoned. Six gunners were hired to man the town's artillery and sixty soldiers were paid 6s a day to defend St Giles' and its choir stalls. Even Willie Thomson the whistler was not forgotten. He got 6s 8d for two nights' playing at the watch.

In spite of the precautions the town was soon overrun and the Reformers left few Catholic buildings undamaged. In St Giles', the forty-four altars that the merchants, the craftsmen and neighbouring lairds had gifted to the Collegiate Church were all destroyed. Even the little nunnery of St Catherine of Siena was not forgotten, though the nuns had been well beloved.

Leith was more difficult to capture, for it was garrisoned by French troops who

were trained in warfare. When the Army of the Covenant advanced on the port, those Frenchmen came out as bold as brass, so a hasty retreat was needed. Eventually an English fleet blockaded the port and starved the garrison into surrender.

Though the Reformers were not very good at the art of war, there was no denying the miracles they achieved in more spiritual battles against the Papists and the flesh-pots of the devil. By the summer of 1560 that fight was in full swing and everything possible was being done to make the punishment fit the crime. Anyone who remained a Papist was put in the stocks at the market cross and afterwards banished from the town. But some compassion was shown towards more venial sinners like harlots, whore-mongers and brothelers. For a first offence they were forgiven, after being dragged along the street in a cart as a public spectacle. It was only after a second offence that they were branded, with a threat of the death penalty if they still persisted.

Soon the death penalty was introduced for adulterers too and that caused a riot in the town. The highly respected deacon of the fleshers was caught red-handed and was lodged in the Tolbooth to await his last journey to the scaffold. The craftsmen rose in arms and, after a pitched battle with the authorities, stormed the prison to set him free. Some were arrested and thrown into the castle dungeons, but it was all straightened out eventually and the deacon went free.

In other ways too, it must be admitted, the craftsmen were a sore trial in those first months of the Reformation. They seemed determined that the old pagan Catholic procession of the Abbot of Unreason should not have to stop. That caused another riot in 1560. The ring-leader was locked in the Tolbooth under sentence of death and his companions not only broke down the prison door. They smashed the gibbet too.

Still, in spite of setbacks, the work of conversion went on. The General Assembly decided to destroy the choir, transepts and chapels of Holyrood Abbey. The Town Council, not to be outdone, removed the figure of St Giles from the burgh arms and substituted a prickly thistle. In the North Loch a pillar was erected, to show the spot where fornicators were to be ducked.

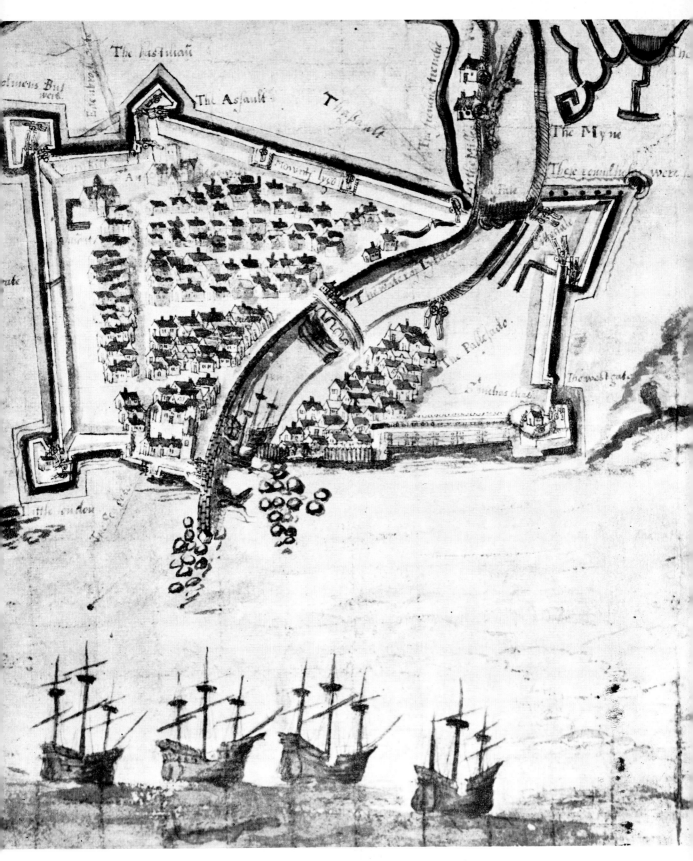

*Only a year before Mary Queen of Scots returned from France English warships were bombarding the port of Leith.*

*Holyroodhouse in 1560, the year before Mary Queen of Scots*
*returned from France.*

[74]

# 7

## Crown of Thorns

IN 1561, Mary Queen of Scots returned to her native land. Few people in Edinburgh had ever seen her, for she was only a child when she sailed for France thirteen years before. But much had happened in the interval. For years she had been an international celebrity. In her infancy she was already Queen of Scotland. When she was fifteen, the great Catholic powers of France and Spain recognised her, instead of Elizabeth, as Queen of England. And in 1558 a third throne came in sight when she married the Dauphin of France.

Not everyone could attend that royal wedding in Paris but everyone could celebrate. In Edinburgh there were pageants and bonfires, with a mighty blast from Mons Meg the biggest thrill of all. Taken "furth of her lair" she was trained towards Granton, and away her gun-stone went soaring high over the cornfields on a journey of almost a mile and a half to Wardie Muir. The man who retrieved the stone and got his reward must have been thankful it was not one of her iron cannon-balls. These had a shorter range of only 1500 yards but they weighed half-a-ton. The stone ones were heavy enough at half that weight.

Only fifteen months after the royal wedding, Queen Mary became Queen of France. If there had been a son by that marriage, he would have become eventually the rightful King of Great Britain as well as France. But her husband's reign was short. By the end of 1560 she was a widow and all that mattered after that was that she was Queen of Scotland. Life for her was beginning to lose some of its glamour. Still only eighteen, she turned her back on the courtly life of France and on 14th August 1561 she sailed from Calais, back to her native land. For the next six years she was to be Catholic Queen of a country that had changed out of recognition since the old exciting days of her grandfather, James IV. Now, in polite circles abroad, Scotland was known somewhat disrespectfully as the arse of Europe. And it was torn by religious strife.

There is a well known painting by a nineteenth century artist of the Queen's arrival at Leith in a ship richly decorated from bow to stern. It shows the quayside thronged with knights in armour, and lords and ladies and commoners. Small boats jostled for a closer view, as she disembarked and crossed a floating platform to the stone steps that led up to the quayside. In the houses in the background, on that sunny day, crowds of onlookers were at every window. And the windows were large and obviously eighteenth century.

It was not only the windows, however, that were not quite right. Other things too didn't quite happen that way. It was in the early morning that the royal ship emerged from a thick East Coast haar, to find only some curious fisherfolk standing around. The reception committee was still asleep in Edinburgh. So the Queen came ashore to the hospitality of a local sea captain's house, while she waited. Sixteen hours passed before she reached Holyroodhouse, just two miles away.

By the end of the day she had won many hearts. Bonfires blazed on the Calton Hill and Salisbury Crags, and

crowds flocked from Edinburgh to see her. They found her entrancing, with her "alluring grace, a pretty Scottishe accente and a searching wit, clouded with myldness". She was, in fact, so enchanting that five or six hundred of her admirers stayed on in the palace forecourt, serenading her with psalms far into the night. But John Knox, the new minister of St Giles', was sorely troubled. "The very face of Heaven," he wrote, "did manifestly speak what comfort was brought unto this country with her — to wit, sorrow, dolour, darkness and all impiety . . . The sun was not seen to shine, ten days before nor two days after."

But the sun burst through on the following Sunday, when she attended her first mass in Holyroodhouse. A band of Reformers, headed by Lord Lindsay of the Byres, forced their way into her private chapel and swept the ornaments from the altar, trampling them underfoot. Their cries of "Kill the priest" so terrified the poor clergyman that, when they were ejected with the altar candles still in their possession, he was scarcely able to conduct the service.

Three weeks later there was a more kindly welcome for the Queen — a grand procession with a truly "pompous show and banquet" in her honour. Almost twenty years had passed since the last State procession along the Royal Mile, so this was a very special occasion. The Queen rode in a triumphal carriage, with young men in taffeta marching in front and twelve sober citizens alongside her carriage, holding a canopy over her head. Doublets of crimson satin could be glimpsed under their black velvet gowns and even their bonnets and hose were of velvet. But everyone, in that long procession, was elegantly dressed to honour the Queen. Without a gown of black silk you could only be a spectator.

Even the route through the town at this black gown procession was rich with sober decorations, "most pompous and magnificent". There were masses of these at the Upper Trone and the Salt Trone,

the Tolbooth and the Netherbow.

The Queen, as she passed along, seems to have taken a good look especially at the pompously decorated Tolbooth. She didn't much like what she saw, for only four months later she sent a letter to the Council, asking them to pull it down before it fell down. There was no mistaking her meaning:

"The Queiny's Majestie, understanding that the Tolbuith of the Burgh of Edinburgh is ruinous and abill haistielie to dekay and fall down, quhilk will be werray dampnable and skaythfull to the pepill dwelland thairabout, and reparand towert the samen, nocht onlie in destructioun of thair houses, bot also greit slaughter of sundrye personis happin and chance thairthrow, without haistie remeid be providit thairin.

"Thairfor hir Heines ordinis ane Masser to pass and charge the Provest, Baillies and Consale of the said Burgh of Edinburgh to caus put workmen to the taking down of the said Tolbuith, with all possible deligence for the causes foresaid, as thay will anser to hir Hienes thairupoun, at hir utmost charge; and so in the mentyme that thay provide a sufficient hows and rowmes reparit as efferis, for the Lords of the Sessioun, Justice and Sheriff ministering of justice to the lieges of the realme.

MARIA R."

After another twelvemonth the Council was spurred to action by the Lords of Session, who threatened to move to St Andrews unless something was done about it. With inflation rampant and unemployment spreading daily, there was no money for expensive new buildings. But on the very doorstep of the Tolbooth the Council found the answer to their problem. A church as large as St Giles' was no longer needed for the town. So the Law Courts were moved into the Holy Blood Aisle, where the merchants' altar had been in the old Catholic days. This part of the church became the High Council-house.

It was a wise decision, for the old Tolbooth did not fall down. It served as a jail for other two and a half centuries. When eventually it was pulled down in 1817, a stony heart was planted in the

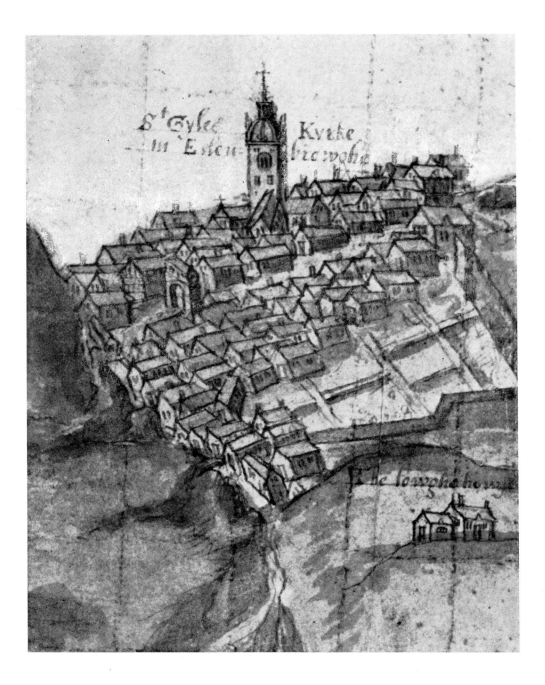

*Edinburgh in 1560, when the town was dominated even more than now by the steeple of St Giles' Kirk. Beside the Netherbow Port is a typically English house of lath-and-plaster but the fact that the artist himself was English may account for that. In the foreground, on the right, is the leper hospital.*

*Mary Queen of Scots would have recognised those buildings in the Abbey Strand, at the entrance to her palace. They were part of the Girth of Holyrood, the largest sanctuary in Scotland.*

road to mark where the unwelcoming doorway of this "Heart of Midlothian" had been.

\*      \*      \*

It took only two years for everyone to start feeling the effects of the Reformation. Not only chaplains and priests had been left penniless. There was a recession too in the building trade, now that the contracts for the Catholic Church had come to a sudden stop.

The authorities, with growing alarm, told the workless to go out and get jobs instead of roaming the streets. No able-bodied man, they pointed out, had a right to beg. And worse than their begging was the fact that they were begetting children and creating the beggars of the future. But, in spite of all this most excellent advice, the unemployment and the pro-creation continued.

Education too was at a low ebb, as the Council pointed out in a letter to the Queen. Seeking permission to build a new school and an old people's home, they emphasised that the whole future of their city depended on education. Without it, no man could serve his country well. And yet, not only in Edinburgh but all over Scotland, it was in decline and no longer given the respect it deserved. People were falling into a barbarous ignorance which was lamentably to be regretted.

The Queen agreed that they should plan for the future, with a school at Kirk o' Field and an old folk's home nearby at the Black Friars monastery. As an added bonus she gave them the grounds of the Grey Friars monastery as a burial place for the town. Until then the dead had been buried round the Kirk of St Giles and downhill towards the Cowgate. But that was creating problems, for the soil was thick with bones.

Well content with their new cemetery, the Council decided to forget meantime about the school and the old people's home. These could wait. So the schoolboys waited fifteen years and the old folk a little longer. But in important matters,

*A stony heart in the roadway*

like the rooting out of sin, not a moment was lost. There was David Pearson, for example. For becoming too friendly with a Canongate servant lass, he spent three hours in the stocks. He was lucky. The girl, her master and the master's family got forty-eight hours to leave the Canongate for ever. If they had still been there on the third day, they would have been scourged out of it.

Even worse than fornication was the risk of people going to Hell in Papist ignorance. Some elderly paupers might well have done that. But they got no alms until they embraced the new faith, and that worked wonders.

Thrawn priests were more difficult. By 1564 there was only one Catholic institution still functioning in the Cowgate, the old people's home with its Magdalen Chapel. So probably it was there that a priest, James Calvert, was caught reading mass "in the Cowgate" one day. He was dragged up to the High Street and locked in the jougs, where he was pelted for an hour with rotten eggs. Even John Knox admitted that the people showed him little mercy.

*The White Horse Close in the Canongate.*

Next day he was tried and found guilty and a huge crowd pelted him for four more hours. Though the sentence was severe, it might have been worse. To remind him that he could have been sentenced to death, the masked hangman, leaning on his axe, stood beside him all the time.

The priest survived his ordeal but one part of it, described to Queen Mary, left a bitter taste in her mouth. Some leading burgesses, she was told, had watched the first part of his punishment, when he was forced to wear the robes for high mass and dragged up to the market cross with a chalice tied to his hands. When the burgesses condoned his being pelted, in such priestly garb, they seemed to be insulting both her religion and herself as Queen.

She was staying at Stirling Castle then but soon afterwards she returned to Holyroodhouse. Compared with the old palace today, the building she knew was much larger and vastly different. Even the great fountain that now stands in the courtyard would have mystified her. She would remember it as the one which Continental craftsmen had made for her father. All her life, it was at Linlithgow Palace. And, in fact, the one at Holyrood now is not the original but a very good copy.

The interior of the palace as it is today would seem strange to her as well. It has lost all its old familiar furnishings.

It was a very different audience chamber that she remembered, with a ceiling three feet higher than now and with tapestries instead of panelling on the walls. Only the heraldic panels and the royal initials still remain and even these have all their bright colours drained away.

The present staircase from Lord Darnley's room up to her bedroom would be unfamiliar too. The one she knew has long been hidden behind the panelling. And even her own bedroom, with its low ceiling, its panelled walls and a seventeenth century bed with faded hangings, is very different from the exquisitely furnished, high-ceilinged room that she once knew so well.

Yet, in spite of the changes, those royal apartments are full of memories. It was in the audience chamber that she had her unfruitful meetings with John Knox. The first was soon after she arrived from France, when she made it clear that she would not be giving up her Catholic faith. A few days later he told his congregation that even a single mass was more fearful to him than the landing of ten thousand armed enemies of Scotland. At another meeting, eighteen months later, he told her bluntly that dancing in the palace lowered its tone and made it look like a brothel. Scotland, she was finding, had standards of morality very different indeed from those she had been taught as a child in France.

The abbey church beside her palace has been roofless now for two hundred years, but it too has its memories. There she married Lord Darnley in 1565. She was twenty-two and two years older than him.

Just beyond the Girth Cross, on the north side of the Canongate, she would be surprised to find how beautiful the White Horse Inn has now become. It was never so lovely in her day. And no doubt, she would be pleased to hear that it got its name in memory of her own white palfrey.

There was one thing that the Reformation did not change. At Christmas only a few months after her wedding, the Provost received a gift from the town of an ox, a tun of wine and thirteen yards of velvet for a civic gown. His colleagues gave £12 Scots of public money for the Provost's Ox, for it had to be the best that money could buy. It was a time-honoured custom. That Christmas, too, the Queen became pregnant.

Six months later, about eight in the evening on a Saturday early in June, she was dining with friends in a room adjoining her bedroom. Her private secretary, the Italian David Riccio, was there — a man more interested in poetry, music and the arts in general than in the

more noble Scottish pursuits of manly feuding and feasting. At the French Court there had been many like him. But in Scotland, as the highest lords in the land would have told you, he was a sad misfit, not even a subject of scandal.

That evening's supper was interrupted by a rustle on the private stair leading up from Lord Darnley's bedroom. The door was flung open and into the Queen's presence rushed a band of armed men headed by the Earl of Morton and Lord Ruthven. Darnley was there too, in the background, slightly drunk as usual. In the excitement, the candlesticks were overturned. By the flickering firelight Riccio was dragged from the table and through the door into the audience chamber. The Queen tried in vain to save him. He died at her feet with over fifty wounds. Lord Ruthven is said to have struck the blow which left Darnley's dagger deep in the dead man's heart.

Three weeks and two days later a sheriff depute of Perth was hanged and quartered for his part in that night's butchery. He had held the Queen captive in her private apartments for forty-eight hours. That day too a priest, turned Protestant, was hanged and quartered as the leader of a mob, five hundred strong, who had burst fully armed into the palace. They stole the keys, locked the gates and even laid violent hands on the Queen herself. But everyone knew that the chief culprits — the lordly ones — remained unpunished.

To Queen Mary it was not just the murder that preyed on her mind. For weeks Darnley had been urging her to give him the crown matrimonial, the right to be King if she died first. The fact that the murder had been staged in her presence when she was six months pregnant left her with a macabre feeling that it was her death even more than Riccio's that he had been seeking.

In Edinburgh Castle, with a moat and drawbridge to protect her against plotters, she gave birth in the autumn to the future James VI, the first ruler of the three kingdoms of England, Scotland and Ireland. The birth took place in a tiny room which still survives with its oak panelling, its coat-of-arms and royal monogram. But these were added later. Even the window is different now. The boards on the upper wall are probably all that survives of the room she knew.

When the baby was baptised at Stirling, in December, the record tells us: "The King came not to the said baptism." By then he was sorely troubled with venereal disease.

The Queen herself had never fully recovered from the shock of Riccio's murder. In the month of the christening a foreign ambassador wrote in his report: "She is in the hands of the physicians, and I do assure you is not at all well; and do believe the principal part of her disease to consist of a deep grief and sorrow. Nor does it seem possible to make her forget the same. Still she repeats the words, 'I could wish to be dead'."

She was then in Craigmillar Castle, a fortress that bristled with defences. Even to this day it still has reminders of her. Only a short distance away is Little France, so called because many of her French friends lived there. Until recently you could have seen, behind a railing at the roadside, the stump of a tree which the luckless Queen planted. It was there for more than four centuries. But a few months ago it was set on fire one night by passers-by and only charred fragments were left.

In the castle itself you can pass through Queen Mary's Door and up the stair in the three-storeyed range to Queen Mary's Apartment, though there is just a little doubt whether in her day this apartment was not in fact a kitchen.

But most people, when they think of the Queen and Craigmillar Castle, find their thoughts turning to the plot which three of Scotland's most powerful noblemen, Argyll, Huntly and Bothwell, concocted. Without mentioning Darnley by name, they signed an agreement that such a young fool and proud tyrant should not be allowed to rule over them and "he

*The South Bridge and South College Street now meet on the site of Kirk o' Field, where Lord Darnley was murdered.*

sould be put off, by ane way or uther". If one of them did the deed, they agreed, all would share the responsibility.

Three months later Lord Darnley was dead. He had returned to Edinburgh in January and moved into the old Provost's House at Kirk o' Field, beside the Flodden Wall. One gable window rested on the wall and a wooden balcony actually overhung it. Today the view is more restricted. The South Bridge and South College Street meet there today.

The house had two bedrooms, one above the other, and the upper one became Lord Darnley's. Tapestries were hung on the walls, a bath was installed and the Queen provided a new four-poster bed, sumptuously draped in black figured velvet. But she had forgotten about the pails of water that had to be carried up and down for his baths. It would have been a pity to spoil a good bed with the steam. So on second thoughts she removed the new one and put in its place an old bed draped in royal purple. Lord Darnley was fond of royal purple. She also had one of the doors removed from its hinges to provide a cover for the bath.

In fact, she could scarcely have been more attentive. Several nights, instead of going back to Holyroodhouse, she slept in the downstairs bedroom at Kirk o' Field. On Sunday 7th February she spent most of the evening with her husband and several lords including Bothwell. There was no romance then between her and Bothwell. But the Craigmillar plot was thickening fast. While they chatted in the gathering darkness, two of Bothwell's servants fetched a grey horse from the stables at Holyrood Abbey, where he had his lodging, and they too set off for Kirk o' Field, with the first of two loads of gunpowder.

Delivering it took longer than had been foreseen and Bothwell came out to find what had gone wrong. Richly dressed in a satin doublet flicked with velvet and trimmed with silver, he strode impatiently up and down, urging them to hurry and be done before the Queen came out and saw them. Actually she did come out but luckily for them she did not look up the garden. As they trudged back along Blackfriars Wynd with their empty portmanteau, they could see her only a short distance ahead, silhouetted in the light of her attendants' torches.

An hour later, Bothwell returned to his lodgings in Holyrood Abbey but after midnight he went back to Kirk o' Field. The gunpowder was stealthily carried into the house. the fuse was lit and then the conspirators slipped away to watch from a safe distance. There was a blinding flash and a deafening explosion. Taking to their heels they fled up Blackfriars Wynd and down a close to a break in the wall at Leith Wynd. Lord Bothwell, who had hurt his hand, was unable to climb over, so they returned to the Netherbow Port and wakened the keeper. He unlocked the gate and let them through.

It was odd that the keeper had slept through the explosion, for it wakened the Queen in Holyroodhouse and at Kirk o' Field it left scarcely one stone on top of another. The mangled body of a servant was found among the rubble. In an orchard just outside the Flodden Wall was the body of Lord Darnley's valet, who had been sleeping in the same room as his master. A little way off, under a pear tree in the snow, lay the body of Darnley himself, clad only in his nightshirt. His dressing gown of royal purple, his slippers and a chair were scattered nearby.

There was no doubt in anyone's mind that Darnley had been murdered, but still there was a three months' delay before the search for the guilty began. That only started after Queen Mary, on a sudden mad impulse, had shocked her friends and enemies alike by marrying Lord Bothwell. It was her third luckless marriage and the most disastrous of them all.

The despised Lord Darnley became a martyr overnight. Posters appeared on the Tolbooth door, denouncing Bothwell as his murderer and the Queen as a

whore. Within three weeks they were out of Holyroodhouse for ever. Another week saw Bothwell a fugitive and the Queen paraded up the Royal Mile through crowds screaming "Burn the whore, burn the parricide!" Next day she was imprisoned in Loch Leven Castle and there Lord Lindsay of the Byres persuaded her to abdicate, with a dagger at her throat. It was the same Lord Lindsay who had led the mob, five years before, that ransacked her private chapel on her first Sunday back in Scotland.

As soon as Queen Mary was in Loch Leven Castle, the search for Darnley's murderers began. That same day Captain William Blackadder was arrested and a week later he "wes drawin backward in ane cairte from the Tolbuithe to the Crosse, and ther wes hangit and quartered for being on the King's murder".

By 13th January, with the round-up far advanced, a great pile of arms and legs was ready for delivery throughout the country. Three boys got fifteen shillings each for carrying some of them to Perth, Dundee, Aberdeen, Elgin and Inverness. Two others set off with a laird's head for Glasgow and legs for Hamilton, Dumbarton, Wigtown and Ayr. They got £4 2s for their trouble. And another boy took the south-east route with more legs for Leith, Haddington and Jedburgh. The creels and wax added another ten shillings to the cost of those ghoulish exhibits.

A few months later, on 2nd May, Queen Mary escaped from Loch Leven Castle and within hours an army was rallying to her support. But Edinburgh was then having its own private war. The craftsmen, defying the church and the law, had revived the old Robin Hood Procession. When the authorities tried to disperse them, they seized the city gates, poured abuse on the magistrates and then, getting completely out of hand, attacked and robbed any country folk they found on the streets. Breaking into the Tolbooth they set the prisoners free, then dragged out the gibbet and smashed it in fragments. Finally, with guns and stones, they bombarded the magistrates in the Council House until a solemn promise was wrung from them that no one would be prosecuted. That was the last time the burgesses tried to pass to the wood to bring home the summer.

*Edinburgh Castle from the Grassmarket.*

# 8

## A Vanishing Landmark

WITHIN A few days Queen Mary's bid to regain her throne foundered in the battle of Langside. But Edinburgh had an aftermath that continued for six more years, before it finally came to an end amid the smoke and din of battle. When the smoke eventually blew away, one of Edinburgh's most familiar landmarks had vanished too.

The trouble began when Kirkcaldy of Grange, the captain of Edinburgh Castle, decided not to support the authorities and the child King James, but to be on the Queen's side. For a long time he kept this a closely guarded secret, while he quietly made his preparations. It was only in 1571 that the Town Council realised what was happening. Under their very eyes he had been strengthening the castle until it was equipped like an arsenal. In February that year he took over a merchant's house on the Castle Hill and transformed it into a guardhouse. By April he was building up his armaments with regular supplies of munitions from France and that month too, in a sudden swoop, he seized all the weapons that the town possessed and carried them off to the castle. By then he had far more than he would ever need for defence alone.

He was gaining support all the time. In Edinburgh many burgesses were beginning to think they had treated the Queen too harshly. Kirkcaldy was able to get provisions and supplies whenever he wanted them, from local merchants, in spite of the Council's efforts to stop them.

Unhappily he had one great fault. He was too much a soldier and too little a diplomat. He turned his guns on the town and that soon put the merchants back on the King's side.

Two great bulwarks had to be built across the High Street to protect the townspeople from the cannon-balls and everyone breathed a sigh of relief when an uneasy truce was arranged. But that was only a brief respite. It expired on Hogmanay and Kirkcaldy refused to renew it. Early in the morning of New Year's Day his guns again began to bombard the town. Trade at the fish-market was already in full swing, when a cannon-ball landed among the crowd, scattering them in all directions. Shoals of fish, blown skyhigh, ended on the surrounding rooftops and people flocked from nearby houses to seize the rest, while the confusion lasted. That was an ill move. Another cannon-ball landed among them, leaving five dead and about twenty badly wounded.

The guns left a trail of damage all over the town. The thatched roof of a house at the West Port was set alight and a gale-force wind spread the flames like wildfire. Another shot set a corn stack ablaze in the Canongate. Many townspeople who had been on Kirkcaldy's side that morning loathed his very name before the day was done. But still there was more than a chance that his show of strength would bring the real support he needed, from elsewhere.

Queen Elizabeth, well aware of that danger, sent an army of 1500 foot soldiers and a formidable array of artillery to force him into surrender. After three weeks of incessant gunfire, the English were able to begin the hand-to-hand fighting. At the end of another

*A graven image of John Knox looks out from his old Kirk of St Giles*

week, with five batteries bombarding the castle day and night, a large part of King David's Tower, one of the principal landmarks of Edinburgh, crashed to the ground in ruins. Two days later a further fall choked the great well and the defenders were left desperately short of water. Still, for several more days, the fight went on until at last Kirkcaldy accepted an honourable surrender. The Regent Morton soon forgot the honourable part of it. He executed Kirkcaldy and several of his companions, including James Mosman the silversmith.

Peace returned to Edinburgh after that, though the fear of future bombardments was not quite set at rest. By the following year a massive Half-Moon Battery was rising out of the ruins of King David's Tower, with its guns glowering down on the town. When that was

finished, not a trace was left of the ruined tower house of the Kings of Scotland.

By the end of last century no one could say with certainty whether even the foundations of the old tower had been left. But then there came the suggestion that part of it was still there, deep beneath the battery. In 1912, excavations proved the rumours true. The long lost tower was rediscovered. It had been sixty feet high in its heyday and part of it still reached a height of fifty feet, with gunloops still menacing the town. It must be the only time in history that a castle, fifty feet high, has got lost. But strange things have been happening all through the ages at Edinburgh Castle.

While the Half-Moon Battery was being built, another old familiar landmark was losing its familiar look. An extra storey was erected on top of St Margaret's Chapel and the whole building was turned into a gunners' storehouse.

John Knox by then was dead. For many months his strength had been failing, though the fire was in his sermons to the end. He died about the time when the bulwarks were being built across the High Street, just beside his church.

One day we shall know how well the seeds he sowed bore fruit in the courts of Heaven. But we can be sure that with all his effort there was an almighty jump in the number of good Scots accents around the heavenly throne and droves of Papist "Whores of Babylon" must surely have gone tumbling headlong down from there to Hell.

His earthly achievements, too, live on. Without a shadow of doubt, God was brought into scores of Edinburgh houses, visibly, for all to see. In the display of piety, burgesses vied with their neighbours as never before. Down the closes and up the Royal Mile, there was a Godly welcome wherever you went. No house was complete without at least one pious inscription above the doorway to greet you as you entered. Many of the lintels with their inscriptions still survive.

"Feare the Lord & depart from evill"

*Huntly House—"The Speaking House"*
(*Now Edinburgh's principal local museum*)

says one, with a slightly reproving air. Another, in Blackfriars Wynd, exclaims: "O Lord, I put my trust in thee. Let nothing work me harm." And in the Old Bank Close is another not unlike it — "In Thee is all my trust 1569."

For many years this Godly air persisted. Even the master tailors were inspired with it in 1621, when they built themselves a new meeting place in the Cowgate. Above one of the doorways of this Tailors' Hall you can still read:

To the Glorie of God and Vertewis renowne
The Cwmpanie of Tailzeours within this good tovne
For meiting of thair craft this hal hes erected,
In trvst in Gods goodness to be blist and protected.

But the Achesons in the Canongate were less conventional. In 1570 they enlarged a house that had been there for many years. Bringing its frontage forward into the street, they erected a facade of hewn stone, with three great timbered gables above. Some people seem to have suggested they were being too extravagant. So it got four inscriptions instead of one — two of them pious and the others more earthy. In elegant Latin one of these blandly told the critics "I don't need to listen to you," while another added: "It's mine today and yours to-morrow, so why are you worrying?"

For a long time this Acheson house was known as the Speaking House, because of those inscriptions. But it also bore the grander name of Huntly House, a title it scarcely deserved, since it never was the town house of the powerful Huntly family.

\*       \*       \*

Housing accommodation in Edinburgh was becoming hard to find by that time. One Frenchman could remember no other place where people lived so close-packed together. And since no one liked the idea of enlarging the boundaries of the town, new houses were tending to be built much higher than the ones they replaced. There was such a demand for stone that the quarries around Browns-field on the Burgh Muir were no longer able to supply enough. By the end of the century another quarry was opened in the King's Park and, three years later, yet another at the Calton Hill. Most of the new houses were of stone. Many were of freestone. And they would have made a fair show, said Fynes Morison in 1598, had it not been for their wooden galleries. These were still almost universal along the Royal Mile.

Not only houses were being built, however. In 1591 the courtly inhabitants of the Canongate took down their ruinous Tolbooth and replaced it with a new one more suitable for that exclusive village. "Great and sumptuous," it was described at the time, with its fine bell-tower above a vaulted pend.

In Edinburgh too, progress was in the air. In 1578 the Town Council built their long-delayed High School on ground that had once belonged to the Black Friars. Two years later, still more ambitiously, they provided a "Tounis Colledge" for advanced education, the forerunner of the University of Edinburgh. It was opened in 1583 with eighty-four students and a strict code of rules. "Early to bed and early to rise" was the golden one. In summer the first class of the day was at 5 a.m. and in winter only one hour later. Students had to wear gowns at all times, and speak only Latin and frequent neither taverns nor funerals. But in their more active pursuits, at least, they could mingle with the dead. Their playing-field, out near Causewayend on the Burgh Muir, was called the Gallow-Green because at one corner was the public gallows, once with as many as nine corpses dangling from it.

\*       \*       \*

People tended to be more superstitious then than now and even royalty was not immune. A few hours before Mary Queen of Scots was executed in 1587 she wrote to her brother-in-law, the King of France, enclosing her two healing stones

as her dying gift. Faith in stones like these was widespread until a century and a half ago and many vouched for the cures they wrought. Some stones had to be rubbed on the trouble-spot; others were stirred in water; and small ones were often worn round the neck for prevention or cure.

About the time of Queen Mary's execution, the Countess of Crawford had a stone that cured leprosy if you hung it round your neck for five days. This was one of several well-tried remedies that Janet Stewart acquired from her. Janet's whole life was devoted to healing the sick and her Canongate house had many such treasures. In her knowledge of herbs, poultices and draughts she had learned a great deal from Damiet, the well known Italian enchanter. But it was a smith in Lasswade who gave her the remedy that brought her good work to its culmination.

When a certain Bessie Inglis in the Cowgate became critically ill and all ordinary treatment failed, Janet was turned to, in a last desperate bid to save her life. She took a petticoat that the dying woman had worn, and dipped it in a south-running stream. Then, when it was still soaking wet, she put it on the woman, while murmuring over and over again "In the name of the Father, the Son and the Holy Ghost." After that she burned some straw at each corner of the bed and, to the amazement of all who heard of it, from that moment the woman began to recover.

There were not many in Edinburgh who did not hear of that marvellous cure. Even the authorities were impressed. It was only too clear, of course, that Bessie Inglis was going to have her problems in the hereafter. Janet had obviously been using witchcraft. She had sold the poor woman's soul to the Devil and, when death did eventually come, there would be no escape from Hell. It was a dreadful thing to happen in a civilised God-fearing country.

So, to prevent the like again, they strangled Janet Stewart and burned her body to ashes.

Catherine Campbell, another "wytch-wyfe dwellan in the Canongate", met a similar fate. There was Sir Lewis Bellanden too, Lord Justice Clerk and one-time Ambassador to England. No less an authority than Sir John Scot tells us in his "Staggering State of Scots Statesmen" that one day in 1591 Sir Lewis brought the noted wizard Richie Graham to his mansion in the Canongate to cure him. And certainly the result was staggering. The wizard raised the devil in the courtyard and Sir Lewis died of fright. There was no doubt it was the devil. That was accepted as beyond dispute, at Graham's trial, before he was burned at the market cross.

Witches and wizards, however, were not the only people who were depriving Edinburgh's medical profession of its just rewards. Some French surgeons were finding it profitable to leave their native land and practice in Scotland instead. Among these was a certain Awin, a man with a high skill and a fine reputation. His only fault was that some of the operations he performed could have been done just as well by the Edinburgh surgeons. So the Town Council decided that he must restrict his work to cutting for stones, curing ruptures, cataracts and the pestilence, and treating distempers of women after childbirth. If he went beyond these he was liable to imprisonment and a fine of £20 Scots for each offence.

He was soon able to try his skill on the pestilence, for in 1585 Edinburgh had its worst outbreak since the Black Death in the fourteenth century. A woman brought it home with her to the Fishmarket Close, after a visit to Perth, and her death in April marked the start of an epidemic that spread rapidly through the town.

The Earl of Arran was Provost then. With James VI he fled to Dirleton Castle, where they passed the time not too unpleasantly, banquetting and staging one of those Robin Hood pageants that had been banned by Church and Parliament alike. But the revels came to a sudden end, after they had been there twelve

*The Gallows was moved to where Preston Street School now stands.*

days. The Earl turned deadly sick. The young King forbade him or his family to set foot out of the castle, and then with all speed he hurried away to Stirling.

Meantime the plague huts were going up again on the Burgh Muir — some around the deserted nunnery of St Catherine of Siena but most at the foot of Blackford Hill, between St Roque's Chapel and the present Canaan Lane. The sick were not always content to stay there like law-abiding citizens but usually the attendants were a bigger cause of trouble than the patients. A gibbet stood beside the huts to deal with any trouble, and there two attendants were hanged in June for stealing clothes from sick folk. Even the "foule hangman" had to be fastened in irons to his own scaffold for a misdemeanour soon after his appointment.

That, of course, was not the only gibbet on the Burgh Muir. There was the other one nearer the town, at the corner of the college playing fields. Not long before, this one had been modernised by heightening the surrounding wall, "sua yt doggis sal not be abill to cary ye cariounis furth of ye samyn as thai hes done in tymes past". A year after the plague, this gallows was moved nearer the town, to where Preston Street School now stands at the corner of East Preston Street.

Leprosy was almost more dreaded than the plague and in Edinburgh it persisted longer than in most Scottish towns. In 1591, when it had almost disappeared elsewhere, a new leper hospital was provided by an Edinburgh merchant, on the site of the old one that the Carmelite friars had run for almost forty years before the Reformation. It was at the north-east side of the Craigend Gate, just east of the pathway to Leith.

The five leper patients took it in turn to sit each day at the hospital door, sounding a clapper as they begged for alms. The wives of two of them also lived there and did the household tasks, and one of the wives was allowed to do their shopping at the market. But, apart from that, the rules were the same for wives and husbands. If they went away from the hospital or allowed any friend or relative to visit them there, or left the door unlocked between "the downpassing of the sone and the rysing thairof", the penalty was death. And, just in case they might ever forget that, at their doorstep they had their own private gibbet where they could be hanged without ever leaving their home.

Infectious diseases were not the only ills that the authorities had to combat. Fiery tempers were sometimes an even bigger problem. High and low alike had an uncontrollable itch to go around shedding blood. Even the High School pupils had it, though the oldest of them were scarcely into their teens. Armed with swords and pistols, they rose in revolt in 1587 and locked themselves in the school. After the magistrates had broken down the door, the eight ringleaders were thrashed as an example to the rest and fined to meet the cost of the damage. The rules too were tightened. In all time coming there was to be only one holiday in the year, from 15th to 22nd May.

The nobles also had been setting a bad example, so that same year James VI made a bold bid to turn their hatred into love. At Holyroodhouse he held a banquet for the wildest of them and followed it up with an after-dinner talk on the virtues of friendship. Next day he led them two abreast, each holding the hand of a mortal foe, in a colourful procession up the Canongate to the market cross. But even that had no lasting effect. The slaughter continued as an almost daily occurrence.

Schoolboys and nobles were not the only offenders. Next year the crafts were involved in a riot more ugly than usual for them, when the sons of some master craftsmen with the help of some unfree journeymen tried to murder one of the bailies in his house. Luckily it was realised at the trial that the sons of the master craftsmen were as innocent as new-born babes. The unfree journeymen

— "vagabonds of wicked lives, rioters and disturbers of the public tranquility" — were the cause of all the trouble. So they were banished with their wives and children.

*        *        *

In those days the trade of Edinburgh was expanding so fast that even the most experienced travellers were astonished. The Duc de Rohan described the town as the busiest commercial centre in Scotland, and Taylor the Water-Poet was equally impressed. Leith alone, said Taylor, was exporting about a third of a million English bushels of wheat, oats and barley each year — to Spain, France and other foreign parts. And yet grain was also being exported all along the Fife coast and as far north as Aberdeen. It made him wonder that a kingdom so populous "should nevertheless sell so much bread-corn beyond the seas and yet have more than sufficient for themselves".

It was not just grain that the Edinburgh merchants were sending abroad. To Campvere and Bordeaux went the fleeces of sheep and the skins of otters, badgers and martens. Other French ports were always willing to take linen and woollen cloth, fleeces and goatskins, and smoked, dried and salted fish. The Baltic ports were interested mainly in clothes and skins. From all these goods the merchants made their fortunes. But the craftsmen were not just interested in money. They took pride in what they produced. Some of the silversmiths, in Edinburgh and the Canongate, were famed for the quality of their work—for their mazers especially, which were exquisite enough to grace the tables of the noblest in the land. And the pistol-makers in the West Bow were scarcely less renowned. They had an international clientele.

Imports, either then or later, included a surprise item from South Norway. Botanists will tell you of one potentilla, *P. norvegica*, which is quite common in Norway but entirely unknown in Britain, except at the Leith docks. What started off as a stowaway seed in a shipment of timber from Norway to Leith has settled down happily at the quayside to become what the botanists would describe as one of the rarest of Britain's adventive flora.

But even being an ordinary Edinburgh merchant was exciting enough in those days. It opened the floodgates not only to financial success but to a whole new world of etiquette as well, with refinements undreamt of before. Robert Vernour managed to burst into that new world in 1588, when he abandoned his old trade as a skinner to join the ranks of the merchant gild. Very soon he got a stern reminder from his new-found brothers that for the honour of the gild his wife and servants must no longer go out to the street in their aprons.

In the latter years of the century the richest of all the Edinburgh merchants was Bailie John McMorran, who specialised in the export of grain, to Spain and elsewhere. He was not entirely popular, for his exports continued even when they caused a shortage at home. Some local ministers tried to persuade him that his fellow-townspeople came first. But they never quite managed to convince him. After all, he needed the money, for his handsome mansion in Riddle's Court was expensive to maintain.

Four centuries have passed since he lived there but still it is as charming as ever. By its very style you can tell he was a man of substance and a big spender. The walls and ceilings were painted. The dormer windows, with wooden shutters on the lower half, had the rare luxury of glass above. And since the first Scottish glassworks, at West Wemyss in Fife, had not even begun production, those window panes were certainly imported — most likely from France. Another sign of quality was the indoor sanitation — the garderobe near the entrance to one of the larger rooms.

There were no fewer than seven doors snuggling together in the little court in front of his house. A pend leads from there to an outer court and the Lawnmarket beyond. Above the pend is

the inscription "Vivendo discimus" (We learn by living). But Bailie McMorran also learned by dying — that it is dangerous to meddle with angry young schoolboys. His last duty as an Edinburgh bailie was at the High School. The boys, still getting only one week's holiday in the year, staged a sit-down strike in protest and he was sent to stamp it out. He ordered the town officers to burst the door open and a moment later he fell dead, pierced through the brain by a pistol shot from a classroom window.

The boys were nearly lynched in the first blaze of anger but calmer counsels soon prevailed. Though Bailie McMorran was a very important person, the small boy who fired the fatal shot was of even better stock. The lordly Sinclairs of Caithness had spawned him. So the indiscretion was overlooked and he grew up to be Sir William Sinclair of May, ancestor of the Earls of Caithness.

It was a pity that the bailie couldn't have lived just two more years. In 1598 his house was used for one of the biggest social events of the year — a grand banquet at which James VI, Queen Anne and her brother the Duke of Holstein were entertained "with great solemnity and merriness". He would have liked that.

*The Royal Mile*

# 9

## "One Very Fair Street"

IN 1603 Queen Elizabeth died and James VI rode south to be James I of England. London was not so very far away. "I shall visit you every three years at the least, or oftener as I shall have occasion," he promised his Scottish subjects. In the twenty-two years of his reign over Britain, he only once made a brief return visit.

Many a nobleman too gave up his town house in the Canongate to enjoy the more sophisticated court life of London and many an Edinburgh burgess found financial reasons for joining in the southward drift. George Heriot was one of those burgesses. In his Edinburgh days he ran an exclusive moneylending business from an office scarcely more than eight feet square, in the Luckenbooths, and so he belonged to the goldsmith branch of the Hammerman gild.

The highest in the land were among his clients. A letter still survives that Queen Anne sent him, when she was going off to Stirling: "Gordg Heriott, I ernestlie desyr your present to send me tua hundrethe pundis vithe all expidition becaus I man hast me away presentlie.— Anna R." She was one of his good reasons for going to London, for in 1603 she owed him £50,000. The King too could rely on "Jingling Geordie" in any emergency and the Edinburgh financier got his reward in the end. He died a very rich man. In his lifetime he had his sorrows. His two sons were drowned on a voyage from Scotland to London. When he died in 1624, the townspeople learned to their amazement that he had left them a legacy of £23,625 to build a school where young people would

learn the Arts and Sciences. So, in course of time, Edinburgh got its Heriot's Hospital. An early writer described it as "stately like a palace" and he was not exaggerating.

Another who made the journey south was Gilbert Primrose. Though he attained the ripe old age of eighty before he died in 1616, you can still read on his monument in Greyfriars Churchyard that to the end of his life he was "principal surgeon to James and Anne, Monarchs of Great Britain, France and Ireland".

It was not easy, however, for the people of Edinburgh to accustom themselves to a Royal Mile without royalty and a palace stripped of its furnishings. Only a few months after the King's departure, the Earl of Montrose was sent to Holyroodhouse to make an inventory of what was left. Apart from a clock, a few pieces of tapestry, part of a bed and a chair covered with purple velvet, there was practically nothing. Even the King's lions had been removed from their den at the back of the palace. Some of the richness of Edinburgh life was gone forever.

So, when news arrived some twelve years later that King James was planning a return visit, all possible steps were taken to make it the first of many. In 1615 the preparations at the castle began. Well over a century had passed since its royal suite was built and it was long out of date. Now it was remodelled in Renaissance style regardless of cost. For upwards of two years the work went on. Hewn stone was brought from the quarry at Innerleith Craig and from another west of St Cuthbert's Church. The sand and

sea clay were from Leith and the lime from Kirkliston, while Newhaven supplied the oyster shells that were used for pinnings. Three ships brought the larger beams from London. Orpington and Danford provided the oak, elm and ash. And the iron, of course, was from Sweden and Dantzig. Sculptors were employed to carve royal monograms on the window pediments and there was danger money for the masons "in consideration of their dangerous standing upon ladders". Some fine blue ribbons were purchased too, to decorate the castle keys which were to be presented to His Majesty.

Shortly before the King's arrival, his bed was sent up from London. John Sawyers got £16 13s 4d Scots for painting it in all manner of colours. A cookhouse too was specially made and a French chef installed in it, to provide His Majesty with a constant supply of sweetmeats. Mons Meg, in spite of her ponderous weight, was moved to a place of honour. Thirteen sturdy porters were needed for that.

The old gun had become quite a celebrity, with a growing folklore of its own. When Taylor the Water-Poet arrived next year he was told that a child had once been conceived in it. Not easily convinced he crept inside and lay on his back to see. It satisfied him there was room inside and to spare, for someone bigger than him. But Mons Meg had other more important uses. Its real purpose was to toss balls of fire at attacking armies and to open fire with its cannon-balls if the castle defences were breached.

The castle was not the only place where preparations were being hastened for the King's arrival. Down in the High Street the civic fathers were having a look at their market cross. It was showing signs of wear, so they demolished it, very carefully, to avoid any damage to its forty-foot pillar. Since its earliest days the cross had stood on that site but now it was moved farther down the street. It took about a month for the stone masons to build its new body and then a squad of burly seamen was brought from Leith to ease the ancient pillar into its modern setting.

The Netherbow Port too was changed out of recognition. The ruinous one that the King remembered was no longer there. Its place had been taken by an infinitely more handsome archway, two storeys high, with a lofty spire in the middle and towers and battlements on each side of the gate. But the new Port was not built for the royal visit. It had been there since 1606.

Only one small detail caused a moment of panic. Statues of apostles and patriarchs were sent up from London by the King, to decorate his chapel. It was enough to make John Knox birl in his grave and it nearly caused a riot. But the trouble soon blew over, for the King graciously agreed that they need not be erected.

Apart from that, the arrangements were an unqualified success. Even the English nobles who accompanied the King were satisfied that during their five weeks in Scotland they were magnificently entertained. James VI, in all his life, was never so eulogised and by all accounts he loved it. Wherever he went he was greeted with long speeches, extolling his virtues in various tongues — English, Latin, Greek, even Hebrew by one small boy. Next year the speeches were published in a commemorative volume that ran to no less than 308 pages. But, despite all that, King James never returned to Scotland.

Charles I also preferred England. His only State visit was in the summer of 1633 for his crowning in Holyrood Abbey. Before his arrival, workmen were sent to the Dalkeith Road to dismantle the gallows and get rid of a corpse on it, in case that struck a jarring note. And so he was welcomed with a great procession, through streets hung with carpets and tapestry. There were 240 youths in white satin doublets and black velvet breeches.

That night a banquet was held in the Great Hall of the castle and next day was

*The Netherbow Port*

the coronation. But more memorable was what Charles I did to the Kirk of St Giles. Part of it was then being used as a Tolbooth, where the Town Council and the law courts had their meetings, while the rest was partitioned off to form three separate churches. The King told the Council to remove the partitions and turn the building into a cathedral church. So for the next five years, the only years in its long history, the Kirk of St Giles was St Giles Cathedral. It was all very inconvenient. You couldn't have three churches and law courts as well in a building without partitions. Two new churches had to be built for the homeless congregations. Everyone thought it a shocking waste of money.

Though the new churches seemed quite needless extravagance, the town itself looked prosperous enough. We have already seen that, fully a century earlier, foreign travellers were enthusing over the beauty of the High Street and the Canongate. They still did so, all through the seventeenth century. In 1618 Taylor was sure it was the fairest and goodliest street his eyes had ever beheld. Sir William Brereton, who cast a jaundiced eye on most things Scottish, described it in 1636 as the glory and beauty of the city, the broadest and longest street he had ever seen. And in 1639 James Howell could remember only one street that surpassed it. That other one was far away, in the Sicilian town of Palermo.

What impressed Sir William especially was the fact that, though the street was about a mile in length, only the channel down each side was left unpaved. It was the broadest, largest and fairest pavement he had ever seen for walking, riding or driving. The middle was always thronged with people, for that was the market-place, the promenade for gentlemen and the exchange for merchants. No matter how heavy the rain, within minutes the surface underfoot was dry again.

Taylor was more impressed by the buildings. As in most medieval towns, the houses overlooking the market place were those of the merchants and master craftsmen. Running steep downhill on either side were scores of closes, some public, some private. Many of the unfreemen lived in the public closes, while in the private ones were the mansions of the aristocracy and the wealthiest of the townspeople, with their families of retainers. Time has proved that Taylor was right when he said the mansions in those private closes, with walls eight feet thick, were "not built for a day, a week or a month or a year, but from antiquity to posterity, for many ages".

But the merchants' houses facing the market place were substantially built too and the newest ones were much taller than in the previous century. Built of dressed stone, they were soon to be five, six and even seven storeys high.

Only one thing, in Sir William Brereton's opinion, prevented the street from being the most stately and graceful he had ever seen. Not a single glass window was in sight. The stone frontages were hidden behind wooden boards, pierced with round holes "to the proportion of men's heads". If the boards had been removed and the height of the houses made uniform, there was no doubt it would have been the most complete street in Christendom.

Those wooden facings also intrigued another Englishman, an anonymous writer who came to Scotland with James VI in 1617. He was left with a vivid picture of the merchants' wives peeping every now and then through "the ventilation holes of their wooden cages" for a breath of fresh air.

The wooden fronts, with their peep-holes, are clearly visible in a bird's eye view of Edinburgh, drawn in loving detail by James Gordon of Rothiemay in 1647. He showed the Canongate Tolbooth with windows. Occasionally, too, high on some tenement there was a dormer window, in marked contrast to the rows of peepholes below. But these were rare. Almost every house from end to end of the Royal Mile was hidden behind its wooden cage.

Not much daylight got into those

*Gledstane's Land*

wooden-fronted houses. But the interiors were full of colour when the lights went on in the evening. Often the walls and ceilings were brightly painted with flowers and fruit, birds and arabesques. And though the colours might seem garish in the full light of modern times, the softer lighting of those days made them altogether pleasing. It was a fashion which the merchants brought back from Southern Norway in the late sixteenth century and it remained in vogue for only about fifty years.

During that half-century Thomas Gledstanes was modernising an old house on the north side of the Lawnmarket. In doing so he created one of the first of Edinburgh's high flats, rising to six storeys. On the ground floor he put in an arcaded frontage. There were several like it, thirty years later, when Captain John Slezer made his drawing of the Royal Mile. But only Gledstane's now survives. He had the internal walls and wooden ceilings painted brightly too, in the prevailing fashion. A knight, a minister and a merchant were among his tenants after the alterations were finished.

Painted ceilings went out of fashion, when the art of the plasterer came to Scotland. Plaster ceilings were much less colourful but far more magnificent than any painting on wood. Among the first to adopt the new fashion was the Dowager Countess of Home. Some of Edinburgh's finest Jacobean plasterwork can still be seen in the mansion she erected in the Canongate, just about the time when Mr Gledstane's high tenement was being built in the Lawnmarket.

When she died, the mansion passed to her daughter, the Countess of Moray, and it has been known ever since as Moray House. Though it has a long and notable history, in its early days it was famous not for its history or even its plasterwork. By far its most outstanding feature then was its garden, which was unique in Edinburgh.

Gardens until then had been places of utility where you grew your apples and pears, and not very good ones, it must be confessed, along with your kale, your herbs and medicinal plants.

If you had travelled north to Scotland from the south of England, you would have known that fruits and flowers became scarcer all the way, until in Scotland they were almost non-existent. The climate was the trouble. You just couldn't expect any variety of flowers and shrubs.

It was about 1630 that this idea was exploded for all time by the garden which Lady Home created at the back of Moray House. David Buchanan had seen her garden. It was so different from any other backyard he had ever seen that he gave it a special mention in an account he wrote of the Edinburgh he knew.

"These gardens," he enthused, "are of such elegance and cultivated with so much care as to vie with those of warmer countries and perhaps even of England itself . . . Scarcely anyone would believe it possible to give a garden so much beauty in this bitter climate."

There were in fact three gardens or terraces at the back of Moray House. On the uppermost the most striking feature was a beautiful thorn tree with drooping branches. Thorn trees were then very popular. On the middle terrace several fruit trees had their branches trained to form a bower. And the bottom terrace had a summer-house or gazebo at one corner, with two lions on top bearing shields. This summer-house was later to play its small part in history.

Also on the bottom terrace was a little pond with the statue of a small boy fishing in it. A bucket of fish was at his feet and an inverted clam shell on his head. An old Latin manuscript tells us that.

Long ago the garden ceased to bear any resemblance to the one which Lady Home created — for gardens, of course, are among the most ephemeral of all things of beauty. But one of its features has survived. When workmen were digging on the site of the lowest terrace, some years ago, they unearthed the original statue of the boy with his bucket and clam shell.

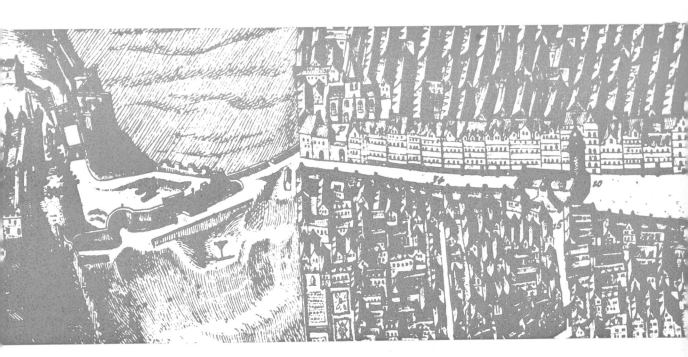

*The Road to the Castle*

# The Royal Mile

IN 1647 James Gordon of Rothiemay drew a Bird's Eye View of Edinburgh which included the whole north side of the Royal Mile. A century had passed since Hertford's raid and the buildings were now much taller, rising in most cases to five or six storeys in Edinburgh itself, though the Canongate mansions were of more modest height.

Here we see the castle, with St Margaret's Chapel on the summit of the rock, and the Lawnmarket stretching eastward. At the top of the West Bow is the handsome new butter market, built on the site of an older one and containing the upper trone. The new market was very soon to be wrecked by Cromwell's troops.

From there the West Bow led down through the West Bow Port, one of the main gates of the city, to the Grassmarket. But to Gordon it was not the West Bow. It was Horse-market Street.

| a | The Castle | 34 | Currers Close |
| b | The Castle Chapel | 10 | The Weigh-house |
| p | The College Kirk | 15 | Horse Market Street |

[103]

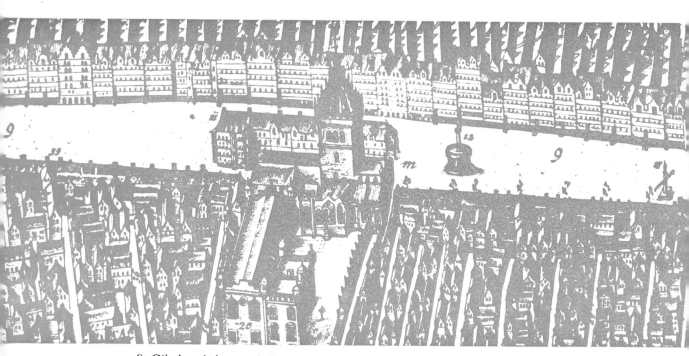

*St Giles' and the new-built Parliament House*

The arches of Thomas Gledstane's house, now the home of the Saltire Society, can be seen on the left. Though now it is the only surviving house in this style, two similar ones are visible in Gordon's drawing.

Dominating the street is the Kirk of St Giles with the Luckenbooths behind, the Tolbooth on the left and the market cross on the right. In front of the church and stretching down towards the Cowgate is Parliament House, then scarcely ten years old.

Farther east is the Lower Trone, close to the still unfinished Tron Church. Beside the church is the Fleshmarket (No. 23), with Marlin's Wynd running along the west side of it, down to the Cowgate.

The Netherbow and its Port mark the east end of Edinburgh. Beyond is the Canongate, with flesh stocks in the middle of the road.

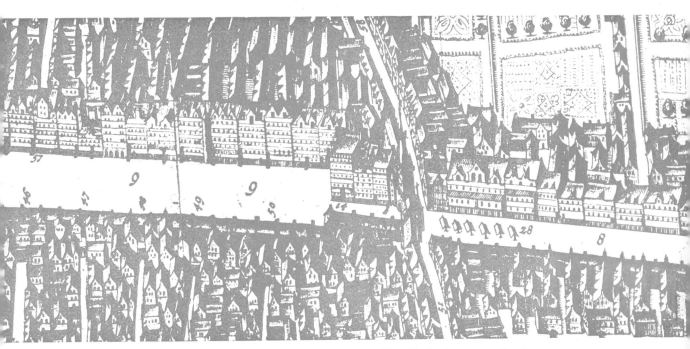

*The Netherbow and the Canongate*

*The Canongate*

The almost complete absence of windows all along the Royal Mile is noticeable. In Edinburgh Gledstane's Land and an occasional dormer high on some tenement, and the Tolbooth in the Canongate, are almost the only exceptions. For well over a century, since the reign of James IV, people had covered the fronts of their houses with wooden facings, pierced with round holes, and the fashion was still almost universal.

Unlike Edinburgh, the Canongate had no high flats and the backyards were much larger.

Just to the left of the Tolbooth, and across the road from it, is the entrance into the courtyard of Moray House. The market cross stands in the roadway and farther down is the Girth Cross, marking the western boundary of the Abbey Precinct, the sanctuary where debtors could live without fear of arrest. Many of those "Abbey Lairds" dwelt there for years in comparative comfort.

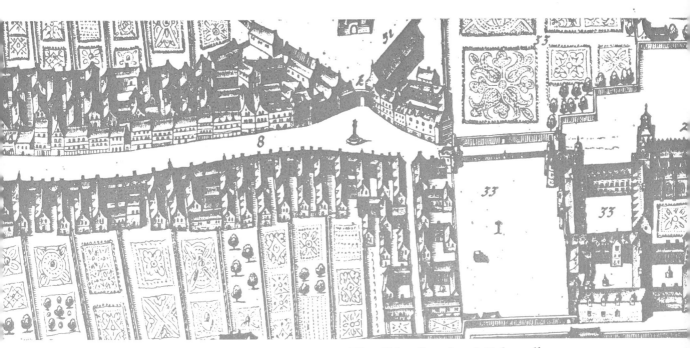

*The Abbey Strand and Holyroodhouse*

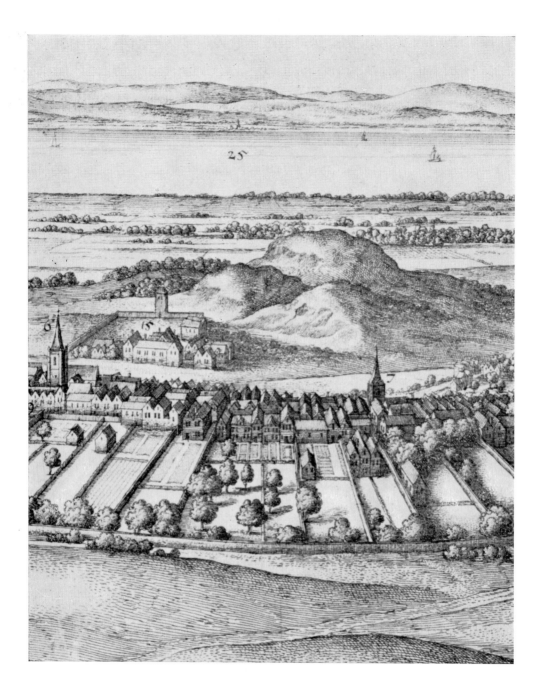

*This detail from Wenceslas Hollar's view of Edinburgh shows Moray House and its garden in the middle. No. 6 is the Netherbow Port, No. 7 the Canongate Tolbooth and No. 15 the Church of the Holy Trinity.*

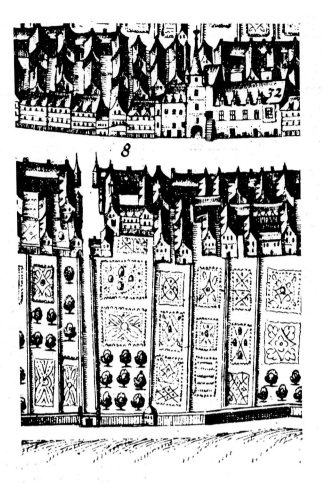

*Gordon's drawing of Moray House in 1647 includes the gazebo at the foot of the garden.*

It might seem odd that this garden should have been described as unique in its beauty, when Gordon of Rothiemay's contemporary map shows a long succession of highly decorative ones all along the Royal Mile. But though Gordon drew his houses with meticulous care, the truth is that his gardens were drawn with no less meticulous abandon.

To find what the one at Moray House was really like, we have to turn to another artist, the Bohemian Wenceslas Hollar, who drew the same scene twenty-five years later. His view is now in Windsor Castle. Not only did he show the Moray garden complete with its terraces. He also made it abundantly clear that the ornate ones elsewhere along the Royal Mile in Gordon's map did not exist.

Moray House differed from its stately neighbours in another respect too. Throughout its history it was the home of Presbyterians, while all around were Royalists. So Lady Home must have enjoyed the exciting scenes in St Giles Cathedral, one Sunday in July 1637. The magistrates and Town Council, with two archbishops, several privy councillors

and the lords of session, were among the huge congregation who gathered that day, to hear the first reading of the prayer book there. It had hardly begun when protests escalated into an uproar. "Dost thou say the mass in my lug?" shrieked one indignant old woman. A moment later the Bishop of Edinburgh hastily ducked to avoid a stool. Even when the rioters were ejected, they battered on the doors and smashed the windows.

Later that day a mob waylaid the Bishop, when he was driving home in his coach. But his footmen slashed in all directions with their drawn swords, and that gave the horses a chance to burst through the crowd and escape at full gallop.

There is no tablet in the church to commemorate that Bishop's lucky escape but the protesters at least were not forgotten. Almost a century ago a simple memorial was unveiled with the words: "Constant oral tradition affirms that near this spot a brave Scotchwoman, Janet Geddes, on the 23rd July, 1637, struck the first blow in the great struggle for freedom of conscience which after a conflict of half-a-century ended in the establishment of civil and religious liberty."

Soon after, the church ceased to be a cathedral. But, with other new churches springing up, how to use the huge building to good advantage was quite a problem. The Presbyterians had always used part of it for non-religious purposes. Like many other burgesses, Thomas Gledstane went there at times, to borrow money on his property. The Earl of Moray's tomb was the place for financial transactions like that. Another small corner was used as a prison and yet another as a weaver's shed. And by 1643 the whole church was sitting on top of a gunpowder magazine down in the vaults. But still it was mainly a place for sermons. By 1669 it had six pulpits and it was reckoned that from each of these you could enjoy as many as thirty sermons a week.

But let us go back to 1637. By that time a new church was being built farther down the street, beside the salt trone and the grave of Jean Marlin. Because it was so close to the public weighing-machine it later became known as the Tron Church. But it was Christ's Church in those days. It was slow in taking shape. The foundation stone was laid about 1637 and, though the first sermon was preached there some ten years later, many more years passed before the roof was finished.

Some decades earlier another church had been built, just across the Grassmarket beside the town's burial ground. It was begun in 1601, on the upper part of the cemetery, and it too was not built in haste. It took twenty years to finish. Like a bride at her wedding this Greyfriars Church wore something old as well as something new. The pulpit came from the High School and the ashlar doorways and buttresses from the ruined convent of St Catherine of Siena.

People took their religion seriously in those days. On Sundays the congregation used to assemble at Greyfriars between 8 and 9 a.m., and for the next three hours they had psalms, prayers and a sermon, with readings from the Old Testament. Many stayed on for the afternoon service and then, after seven hours or more of spiritual food, they went home with a healthy appetite for their first meal of the day.

One service in that church was long remembered. On 28th February 1638 the entire congregation signed a lengthy document telling Charles I how loyal they were but adding that he must no longer interfere with the kirk in Scotland. Other congregations took up the cause. Soon this National Covenant was being signed in churches all over Scotland. But Greyfriars was the first of them all.

A fine new building was going up in the High Street by then — a new Parliament House, close beside St Giles Cathedral. The old one, in the High Council-house inside the cathedral, had not been very suitable. Six courts of justice had been meeting there in far too

cramped surroundings. Fifteen judges, all in purple gowns, sat together on the bench at one of these courts. At another, each of the fifteen presided in turn. "In this Court," said Sir Willam Brereton in 1636, "I observed the greatest rudeness, disorder and confusion that ever I saw in any court of justice; yea, sometimes they speak about two or three several causes at one and the same time, which makes an extraordinary disorder and confusion."

To ease the overcrowding, though perhaps not the confusion, a new building was begun at the top of the slope which led from St Giles Cathedral down to the aristocratic Cowgate. The frontage, towards the church and the new Parliament Close, was only one storey high. But on the other side, where the ground dropped steep towards the Cowgate, it was a building of six storeys with numerous ranges of vaults beneath.

The Great Hall with its lofty arched roof was finished by 1639. There the Three Estates held their meetings, with seats for the lords and bishops and benches for the commoners. At one side was a pulpit the ministers often occupied, and at the other side a throne which the sovereign never used. When the Three Estates met there for the first time, in 1639, they forgot what the National Covenant had said, only a year before, about loyalty to the King. They voted funds for an army to fight him.

Soon, however, the Edinburgh burgesses were to lose their interest in civil war and their fine new Parliament House. In 1645 life suddenly ground to a halt again, as the bubonic plague swept through the city. It was the last major outbreak.

In April the High School pupils were sent home and there were no more classes for the next eleven months. The University moved off to Linlithgow, where the classes were held in the parish church for almost a year. Parliament and the Court of Session left their new home and fled from Edinburgh in July. Even the prisoners in the Tolbooth and the castle were set free to avoid an uprising among them.

Work in the town came to a standstill. A handsome new mansion had been nearing completion on the west side of Brodie's Close, when the outbreak began. Two of the public rooms were to have had decorated ceilings. But only one, with the date 1645, was finished when the workmen withdrew. The other had to wait for a twelvemonth before it was done. To this day you can see the date 1646 on it.

Only a short distance along the street, Mary King's Close ran steep downhill to the North Loch, from just opposite the Kirk of St Giles. The plague raged along it and, when the last of the victims was carried off, each empty house had its tale to tell of that year of terror. Though the close was in the very heart of the city, it was left to moulder into ruins with its ghosts. Eventually it was swallowed up when the Royal Exchange was built on top, a century later. But Mary King's Close still survives, abandoned. Down among the vaulted cellars under the fore-court, it still runs north, until it reaches a grating on a roof in Cockburn Street.

Even when people first began to say that the close was haunted, it was already ancient. A century ago, when one of the ruined houses was being excavated, a carving was found that had been part of a fifteenth century altar in Roman Catholic times. Not inappropriately, it showed a priest performing the last rites on a dying person.

But Mary King's Close was not the only one which suffered during the plague of 1645. The rattle of carts and tumbrils, and the clang of warning bells, became the night sounds of Edinburgh. It was in the hours of darkness that the dead were removed to the burial pits and the sick to the shanty towns that were springing up around the city. Some were taken as usual to the far end of the Burgh Muir. But now there were wooden "ludges" in the King's Park too and the biggest concentration of all was in the grounds of the ruined convent of St Catherine of Siena. There the surrounding walls, almost fifteen feet high, helped to prevent

*The Lawnmarket*

folk getting lost. For centuries afterwards the very mention of Sheens Walls revived memories of the plague.

In Leith the outbreak was so bad that it became impossible to separate the clean from the unclean. In a moving plea to Parliament, one of the bailies begged them "out of the bowels of mercy" to do what they could to help. Leith then was a town of about 4000 inhabitants and fewer than 1600 survived.

While the plague was raging, not many people got a churchyard burial, though a few were decently buried in their own gardens. John Livingston was one of these. A merchant burgess, he fled with his wife out of Edinburgh to his country house on the Wester Burgh Muir and there he died in 1645, while the plague was at its height. The ornamental stone which his widow erected over his grave in Morningside can still be seen in a private garden in Chamberlain Road.

Some folk died less peacefully. It was only natural for parents to hide the fact that their child had been struck by the plague. And so, while they tended the child, they waited in terrified expectation for a knock on the door by a plague official with a white St Andrew's Cross on the front and back of his grey gown. A black-masked executioner could not have inspired more fear. If he discovered the sick child, its mother would be carted off for drowning in one of the Quarry Holes, while the father was hanged at his own house door. People left such houses to fall into ruin, like the ones in Mary King's Close.

Though the plague had been dreaded by everyone, there were some people who just had to live dangerously. Two of these were Mr and Mrs Patrick Watson, who had their home in Dirleton. They had always been suspected of witchcraft and had always denied it. And then, one day, they learned that John Kincaid, the most terrible of witch-prickers, was coming to their village. In a spirit of sheer bravado they suggested that he should search their bodies for the Devil's mark, to settle the rumours for all time. It was the year 1647.

The great hall of Dirleton Castle was the scene of their examination and for a long time the pricking went on without success. But in the end Kincaid found what he was looking for — a spot on each that could be pricked without pain or loss of blood. There was no doubt they were witches. Mrs Watson straightway confessed that she had met the Devil when her daughter was ill. Disguised as a doctor he came to her house and gave her a prescription for which she paid him two shillings. Considering who he was, he really behaved very normally, for he supped some bread and milk that she laid before him and drank some ale that her husband fetched.

The Watsons were by no means the last witches in Scotland but the plague of 1645 was the last of its kind. As the years rolled on, people slowly began to realise that they had lived in one of the great ages of medical progress. Within living memory two of the deadliest diseases known to man — leprosy and the plague—had vanished almost completely from Scotland. There have been miracles of modern medicine but none quite able to overshadow that twofold achievement.

# IO

## Reaching for the Sky

*Holyroodhouse about 1647*

IT WAS in 1647 that Gordon of Rothiemay drew his picture map of Edinburgh. That was the year when Kincaid the Witch-Pricker had his trial of skill with the witches of Dirleton. Oliver Cromwell paid a sociable visit to Edinburgh in the following year, to stay with the Earl and Countess of Moray at their town house in the Canongate.

In 1649 the Marquis of Montrose returned from exile and tried to raise an army in the north, to restore the monarchy. He was captured and brought to Edinburgh, where crowds flocked to the Royal Mile to see him pass in a tumbril driven by the common hangman.

Major Weir and his Town Guard formed the escort.

Earlier that day the Earl of Argyll's eldest son had married a daughter of the Earl of Moray and the wedding feast was in progress as the procession approached. Leaving the table the guests swarmed on to the balcony of Moray House to feast their eyes on the once-dreaded Royalist leader. He gazed back so unconcerned that they shrank away in embarrassment — all except the Countess of Argyll, who spat down in his face.

Two days later Montrose was put to death for high treason. His head and limbs were cut off for display in the

larger towns, and his head for a spike on the city Tolbooth. The rest was buried in a cist under the gallows on the Burgh Muir. And within forty-eight hours the cist was unearthed at dead of night and his heart removed, to be sent in a golden casket to his son in Flanders.

In a few more weeks Scotland was at war with England. But the fighting was soon over. Having routed the Scots at Dunbar, Cromwell marched into Edinburgh and again took up residence in Moray House, this time as a conqueror. Only the castle defied him. The scars it suffered during three months of siege can still be seen on its stonework. When eventually it fell on Christmas Eve, Cromwell made an inventory of its contents and with some feeling he noted that its armaments included "the great iron murderer called Muckle Meg". With more pleasure he then destroyed the royal monograms that had been carved above the window pediments of the King's Lodging, for James VI's visit in 1617.

This was not the only damage done by his troops. Greyfriars Church, the High School and a large part of the University had their "pulpites, daskis, loftis, gaittes, windois, dures, lockes, bandis and all uther thair decormentis . . . all dung doun to the ground by these Inglische sodgires and brint to asses". Holyroodhouse and Greyfriars Church were used to house his army and the still unfinished Heriot's Hospital was turned into a military hospital.

Soon after, on a Wednesday in November, a disastrous fire broke out by accident in Holyroodhouse. Only Queen Mary's apartments escaped undamaged. Eventually Cromwell rebuilt what was lost, but in a style far inferior to the original. The work was scarcely finished when Charles II became King again.

Then, as so often happens, the criminals of yesterday were the heroes of today. And since no one could have been more heroic than the Marquis of Montrose, in January 1661 his remains were collected from a' the airts for the grandest and most solemn funeral that Edinburgh had ever seen. From Aberdeen came one of his legs in a richly decorated casket. His head was removed from its spike on the Tolbooth tower. From Glasgow, Stirling and Perth came his other leg and his arms, and the rest of him from beneath the gallows on the Burgh Muir. Four months they lay in state in the chapel of Holyrood and then, with guns roaring and all the glittering pageantry for which Edinburgh was renowned, they were taken in procession to their last resting place in the Kirk of St Giles. Fourteen earls bore the coffin and twelve other noblemen carried the pall.

There was only one noble absentee, Montrose's old enemy the Earl of Argyll, who was now in the castle awaiting execution. His was a common enough fate in those days. His wife's sedan chair was less common, for it was the first ever seen in the city. The sight of her being carried up to the castle by two brawny clansmen, to visit her husband, started a fashion which survived for almost a century and a half.

\*     \*     \*

With the Restoration of Charles II, Heriot's Hospital was no longer needed as a military hospital and work on it was almost finished. It had taken a long time to build. Few were still alive who could remember George Heriot in his shop in the Luckenbooths, before he went with the King to London. But many could still recall the excitement of the news that he had left £23,625 to provide a school for the sons of the town's poorer burgesses. That kind of money would be worth millions of pounds today and the trustees spent it with a generosity that more than matched the donor's. Regardless of expense they erected one of the grandest Renaissance buildings in Scotland, with a magnificent interior and an exterior so richly ornate that each of its windows — two hundred in all — had its own individual moulding.

In 1661 the first of the pupils moved in and soon there were over sixty blue-

gowned boys learning a trade or studying for the University. Their school put even the University to shame, "There is no one but would at first sight take it for a palace," said Jorevin de Rocheford the year it was opened. But the maintenance was not as good as the design. Scarcely ten years later another traveller bluntly commented that it was a doleful spectacle — "that so noble a heroick design of charity should be so basely perverted to other evil ends and purposes, contrary to the will and intention of the donor".

Though the building itself was being neglected, the more privileged towns-people had no cause to complain. For their exclusive use a promenade was laid out in the grounds of the hospital — a delightful place where a man of feeling could "shun the impertinencies of street fops", as Dr Pitcairne pointed out in "The Assembly", the most popular play of the day. In that same play the hero and heroine had one of their secret meetings there. But an even greater attraction than Heriot's yards was its bowling-green, just south of the school building. By the following century no great mansion in Scotland was complete without its bowling-green. Like the cricket park or the tennis court in later times, it was the place where you could see all the social graces on display. By 1742 there were five exclusive bowling-greens in Edinburgh. But in the 1660s this was the only one.

When the boys were moving into their hospital, another landmark was also nearing completion. A quarter of a century had passed since the foundation stone of the Tron Church was laid at the top of Marlin's Wynd. By 1648 the work was far advanced and an order was sent to Amsterdam for over six tons of copper to cover the roof. But then the plague stopped everything and the arrival of Cromwell's army caused further delay. In 1663 the City Council decided that a green roof was a needless luxury. So, instead of copper, they used lead and slates and the church was soon finished. It had three notable features — a magnificent hammer-beam roof like the one in Parliament House; a curious wooden spire covered with lead; and, for good measure, the most raucous church bell in Edinburgh. "Weel wat I," wrote the poet Fergusson, "they couldna bring waur sounds frae hell."

Yet, just after the Tron Church was finished, something much more discordant than the bell did in fact echo through the streets of Edinburgh — something which had definitely come straight from hell. No less a person than the Devil himself was seen "rattling up the Lawn-market and thundering down the Bow", in a coach that blazed with hellfire. Even the eyes of the coal-black horses were glowing red and fiery.

For that you can blame Major Thomas Weir, one of the godliest men in Edinburgh. Fully twenty years earlier we met him at the head of the Town Guard, leading the Marquis of Montrose on a tumbril up the Royal Mile. Now the major was old and retired, but his godliness had grown with the years. He was a fervent Covenanter, surrounded by no less ardent followers. Major Weir had a wonderful gift for prayer. It had earned him a reputation far and wide.

He lived in a rather handsome house, with a private courtyard in front, a luxury in those days. A close led out to a bend near the top of the West Bow. All day long the tapping of hammers echoed in his ears, for the West Bow was where the coppersmiths, tinsmiths and dagger-makers had their houses, with their workshops beneath. Almost everyone there was a hammerman and almost to a man they were marching along the road to salvation, thanks to "Angelical Thomas". There was sheer extasy at his prayer meetings. People came from fifty miles and more to hear him, in the brotherhood of his dagger-making Bowhead Saints.

Even in his old age Major Weir was still a commanding figure, tall, dark and spare, solemn of countenance and with his gaze turned modestly to the ground. His long cloak made him seem even taller. The hollow ring of his walking stick on the cobbles was like the sound of music.

*Jean was led down the West Bow to be*
*hanged in the Grassmarket.*

He was, in fact, a most respected person. So the shock to his followers was all the greater when one day in 1670 he made the surprise announcement at one of his prayer meetings that he had often committed adultery and bestiality — God forgive him!—and times without number he had indulged in incest with his sister.

For weeks his followers refused to believe him. But eventually the evidence was too strong. Someone remembered that, years before, a girl had been whipped through a west country town for accusing him of just such crimes. His sister Jean, too, not only admitted the incest. She recalled that one night the Devil took her brother and her in his fiery coach with its six black horses from their house in the West Bow to Musselburgh and back. She even reminded them that the major's walking stick was a little unusual. Then they recalled that sometimes, when they visited him, the walking stick opened the door for them. It went

messages too, on its own. And often, when the major was solemnly walking down the Lawnmarket, you would see the stick hopping cheerily on ahead. It had all seemed perfectly innocent at the time, but not so natural in retrospect.

At last one of the Saints told the Provost of Edinburgh about the major's confession. He too was incredulous. Convinced that the poor old gentleman must be deranged, he sent some doctors to examine him. They found him sane and utterly determined to pay for his sins before reaching the hereafter. So on Monday 11th April he was strangled at a stake on the road to Leith and his accursed walking stick was thrown into the flames to be burned to ashes with him. His sister Jean was found guilty too and incest was not her only crime. She had been consorting with witches, especially with one in Dalkeith who could spin at least three times as fast as any mortal woman. Productivity on such a scale was a mortal sin even in those days. So Jean was led in procession out of the Tolbooth and down the West Bow, past her house, to be hanged in the Grassmarket.

The people of Edinburgh did not easily forget their major. His ghost haunted the district long after his death. Many a time it was seen by midnight revellers, usually on foot in the West Bow but sometimes riding furiously out of the close on a headless black horse, to vanish in a sudden burst of flames. Occasionally too the Devil came back in his coach with the coal-black horses, their eyeballs still flashing with fire. There were times when every window in the major's house was ablaze with lights. But the manifestations stopped a long time ago, after the ruins of the house were removed in 1878.

\*    \*    \*

Big changes were coming to Edinburgh about the time when Major Weir died. Next year a massive reconstruction began at Holyroodhouse. Cromwell's handiwork was pulled down and a new facade erected, flanked at one end by the old tower which James IV had erected a hundred and fifty years before.

Edinburgh was going quite Dutch by then. About 1680 there was an invasion of Dutch printers, with their composing frames and presses. They even made their ink the Dutch way, when they printed in huge tomes the Acts of the Parliament of Scotland. By 1684 there were Dutch artists, too, at Holyroodhouse. One of them, Jacob de Wet, painted over a hundred portraits of the Kings of Scotland in a two-year stint that earned him £120 per annum. The walls of the Long Gallery are lined with those tributes to his imagination.

In the Canongate, too, came a breath of fresh air from the Low Countries, for in 1688 a handsome Dutch gable was made a feature of the new Canongate Church.

The whole street was changing. Until then nearly all the houses along the Royal Mile still had their stone fronts hidden behind fir boards, nailed one over another. As late as 1662 these were described by one foreigner as "pierced by round holes, through which the householders put out their heads". But when Thomas Morer arrived in 1689, the Royal Mile was changing fast. It was only in the older houses that you now saw those "oval windows (without casements or glass), which they open or shut as it stands with their conveniency". The newer houses along the street had glass windows, for glass was at last being manufactured in Scotland and was no longer an unattainable luxury. Even in the older houses large openings were now being cut in the wooden fronts to let windows be inserted.

It was not only the arrival of glass, however, which caused this dramatic change in the appearance of the town. From painful experience there was ample proof that the wooden fronts often changed a small fire into a big one. And this was underlined in 1676, when several houses were destroyed in the very heart of the city, at the entrance to Parliament Close. It was a good time for tightening

*Holyroodhouse in 1670*

the regulations. After that, no one was allowed to use wood in building any part of a house. And so the wooden fronts along the Royal Mile began to disappear one by one, as the older buildings were gradually replaced.

In the fashionable Cowgate the change came even sooner. Windows were already there when the Bohemian Wenceslas Hollar made his beautiful drawing of the city in 1670.

Windows were not the only innovation. All the time the new houses were stretching higher towards the sky. You could travel the length of Europe without seeing houses so tall, for these were among the wonders of the world. One Edinburgh bailie, Thomas Robertson, surpassed all the other high flat builders with a block that towered like a giant over the east and south sides of Parliament Close. With fifteen storeys on its Cowgate side, it dwarfed even its thirteen storey neighbours. Bailie Robertson died full of years and was buried in Greyfriars Churchyard in 1686. His mighty tenement survived only a few years longer.

\*       \*       \*

The new high flats were not the only talking point in those days. Lawlessness was rampant too. Over in the West of Scotland the die-hard Covenanters rose in revolt against the King and though they were easily crushed, at the battle of Bothwell Brig in 1679, there were repercussions in Edinburgh. A place had to be found there for almost twelve hundred unrepentant prisoners. Tradition still points to a narrow strip of ground in Greyfriars Churchyard where they are said to have been herded for months, until several died of exposure as winter set in.

Tradition, of course, is sometimes wrong. The prison yard was in fact much larger, extending as far as Bristo

Place, and it contained no graves in those days. The prisoners, too, were provided with huts and, long before winter, the large majority were back home after promising to cause no more trouble. Even the most rebellious had gone by mid-November, on an ill-fated voyage to Barbados. Most of them died in a ship-wreck in the Orkneys.

Five years later the Covenanters were affronted when a statue was erected in honour of Charles II, the monarch they so heartily detested. Like most things in the city, this statue in Parliament Close took a long time to erect. Originally it was to have been of Oliver Cromwell, but he was dead and Charles II back on the throne before the plans were completed. Sensibly the townspeople decided it was better to have a statue of the wrong person than no statue at all. So an equestrian figure of Charles II was erected in 1684, only a few months before his death. It showed him garlanded like a Roman general, sitting proudly half-naked and bandy-legged, on his warhorse. "The vulgar people, who have never seen the like before, were much amazed at it," wrote Lord Fountainhall.

Years later the Covenanters were no longer rebels but they still disliked the statue. Close to the horse's tail they put a stone in the pavement with the letters I.K. and the date 1572, to remind the townspeople that if John Knox was not buried in some other part of the old churchyard he was certainly buried at that exact spot. And since then the statue has undoubtedly had its troubles. Every year, on the King's Birthday, schoolboys used to climb up on the horse to nail garlands on King Charles and in 1824 they did it once too often. The leaden figure collapsed. For eleven years it was stored in the Calton jail and then, strengthened with a wooden skeleton, it was re-erected in 1835. But the troubles continued. Even during the present century it has been repaired three times, the last occasion in 1972, when the horse went knock-kneed under the sheer leaden weight of its royal master. Still, despite

*Left.—Edinburgh in 1670.*

(Windows were now replacing the peepholes of earlier times.)

*The Lost Gravestone*

Latin inscription "The illustrious James, King of Scots, fifth of his name: in the 31st year of his age and the 30th of his reign: died in the Palace of Falkland 14th December, 1542 A.D.: whose body was brought here for burial."

The coffin of his first tragic Queen, the youthful Madeleine de Valois, was there as well, with its crown flanked by gilt fleur-de-lys, and its inscription: "Madeleine, eldest daughter of Francis, King of France: Queen of Scotland, wife of King James V, died 1537 A.D." And there were others too — King David II, James II of Scotland, two royal princes and Henry Lord Darnley, consort of Mary Queen of Scots.

Having inspected the lead coffins they carried off the lids, for these had quite a marketable value, and the royal bones are said to have remained exposed for years to public gaze.

It was odd that this should have happened in Edinburgh, for nowhere in the world were there burgesses who so dearly loved a good honest burial with all the trappings. For almost a century the walls of Greyfriars Churchyard had been acquiring monuments which in their own way were no less unique than the broad High Street and its fifteen storey flats.

This churchyard was one of Edinburgh's showpieces. "It probably not only excels everything of its kind in the open air," said one seventeenth century traveller, "but it vies with many royal sepulchral repositories: Nay, divers of its monuments for magnificence outdo those of many kings which I have seen." And those who had seen the bones of royalty in Holyrood Abbey must have said Amen to that.

Many of the Greyfriars monuments are still worth seeing for their impressive craftsmanship. One of the most ornate— that of Sir Hugh McCulloch—was erected in the very year when the royal tombs were desecrated.

Those merchants of Edinburgh were proud to be men of substance. Among the most stately of the monuments is that of George Foulis of Ravelston, who died

its misfortunes, it has at least outlasted the gravestone. Some five years ago the car park in Parliament Close was given a new layer of tarmacadam and no one has seen the stone since then.

There have, of course, been other accidents in Edinburgh's long history. There was one in 1681, when the future James II paid an official visit to the city as Duke of York. A blast from Mons Meg was fired in his honour — the last blast that the great gun ever uttered, for it burst in the process.

It would not have been needed much longer, anyway. Only seven years later the castle had its last long siege, when James II fled from the throne and William and Mary came over from Holland, in a Bloodless Revolution. From December 1688 the Jacobite Duke of Gordon held the castle for the exiled King and in March next year the Government forces began to bombard it. Three more months passed before they forced the garrison to surrender.

At Holyrood Palace the supporters of William and Mary had more success. In December 1688 they formed a mob that stormed Holyrood Abbey, to purge it of its Roman Catholic ornaments. At the same time they took the opportunity to scrutinise the royal vaults and there they found the coffin of James V with its

[122]

*"The vulgar people were much amazed."*

[123]

about the time when Parliament House was nearing completion. His inscription records that all good people loved him and even among the wicked he had not a single enemy, "despite the ample extent of his own fortune".

Thomas Bannatyne too was a wealthy man when he died in 1635. So his widow was able to order a stone from the same fine craftsman who did the Foulis one. On it we read that though Mr Bannatyne had no children —

> Yet the Lord with meanes him blist
> And on his deare bedfellow
> Jennet Makmath he did bestow
> Out of his lovelie affection
> A fit and goodlie portion,

so she spared no expense in erecting the monument.

There were, of course, some carping critics. "I am sure," wrote Thomas Kirke in 1679, "the pride of this people never leaves them but follows them to their long homes." But it was not mere pride. There was a family spirit too, that gave those merchants an all-consuming urge to finish up, mingled with the dust of their kinsfolk. The Rays are a good example. Their stone tells us that between 1610 and 1808 twenty-eight of them were buried there, including a laird and a colonel, five merchant burgesses, two surgeons, three lawyers, a goldsmith and a schoolmaster. But that is only part of the story. Only men of standing, and a very select number of wives and widows got their names on the roll of honour on "Ray's Tomb". In over two centuries not one spinster or child was recorded.

Even more impressive than the Rays' family plot is the lofty mausoleum of Sir George Mackenzie. A man of vision, he founded what is now the National Library of Scotland and in his duties as Lord Advocate he showed outstanding humanity. He even wrote an essay on tolerance. But, for all his reputation, still he committed one quite unforgiveable sin. In his official capacity he had the job of prosecuting the Covenanting prisoners captured at Bothwell Brig.

He may have slept soundly afterwards but certainly there was no peace for his ghost. People stayed well away from his tomb. It was only many years later that adventurous schoolboys at last began to dance round the building and shout through the key-hole:

> Bluidy Mackenzie, come out if ye daur,
> Lift the sneck and draw the bar.

At least one former pupil of Heriot's Hospital, the son of a stable-owner in the Grassmarket, had reason to bless that haunted tomb. He was sentenced to death for burglary and, while he lay in the Tolbooth awaiting the end, his devoted father planned a daring escape down to the very last detail—even to the extent of acquiring a key that could open the door of Sir George's mausoleum.

To get the lad out of jail was the first step. By a ruse he got rid of one turnkey and persuaded the other to open the outer door. In a flash his son was through it and away. For a time his footsteps could be heard, as he fled down Beth's Close, and then there was silence. Not a trace of him could the authorities find, in spite of all their searching.

A few other people, however, were better informed—among them some boys at his old school. There was only a high wall between them and the churchyard and at dead of night one would come over the wall with the food they had saved during the day. For six weeks they did so, until at last the fugitive escaped abroad and the Lord Advocate lost his room-mate.

Edinburgh in those days had much more than just wealth and pride to commend it. The University was soon to acquire an international reputation for a new and exciting field of research which was now opening up. Until then there had been a certain sameness among the Scottish Universities, a tendency to regard the ministry as the be-all and the end-all of education. Thomas Kirke was as little impressed by those Divinity courses as he was by the pomp of Greyfriars Churchyard. To him it was three or four years

*"A good honest burial with all the trappings"*

*The Haunted Mausoleum*

spent learning little more than graces and prayers: "If you crack a nut, there is a grace for that; drink a dish of coffee, ale or wine, or what else, he presently furnishes you with a grace for the nonce; if you pare your nails, or any other action of like importance, he can as easily suit you with a prayer as draw on a glove."

Now higher education was beginning to spread its wings and Edinburgh was about to gain a place it would retain for centuries, in the forefront of medical research. The time was ripe. In 1681 the doctors of Edinburgh had formed a Royal College of Physicians. And it not only barred all quacks and mountebanks; it also removed many a useless remedy from the shelves of the apothecaries' shops, for these were now inspected twice a year and the useless drugs thrown out.

Four years later the University's medical school began its long and distinguished history with the appointment of two medical professors. That brought no sudden change, for students continued to learn their trade as apprentices of master physicians. For the next thirty-five years the University could offer only a lecture course on botany in summer and chemistry in winter, with the dissection of a human body by the professor of anatomy once every two or three years. But though the medical course was still in its embryo stage, one of the first two medical professors was in a very real sense a pioneer. Sir Robert Sibbald had an absorbing interest in plants at a time when they were still indispensable in medicine.

All through the ages the usefulness of plants had been endless. When household smells were troublesome, as they always were, the rose was prime favourite, especially the Apothecary's Rose, the R. gallica officinalis, which retained its perfume longest of all. At one time every shop in the main street of Provins, in the heart of the rose-growing district of France, was making pot pourri for the export market. But lavender, rosemary and lemon-scented southernwood were effective deodorants too.

There were no psycho-analysts, so yarrow was used to cure depression and, if sleep came slow, some dried leaves of southernwood under the pillow. Yarrow was also invaluable for superficial wounds, though for deep ones St John's Wort was better.

For illnesses there were all sorts of herbal remedies. Fennel seeds steeped in water were useful for a sore stomach, while for epilepsy the root of paeony was "far above all else". An infusion of sage was good for anaemia and soapwort for jaundice, while water cress was widely recommended for scurvy. For a child with whooping cough, Creeping Jenny boiled in red wine with honey was a potent remedy, and so was hollyhock tea for tuberculosis and bladder infections.

Several of the herbs had more than one use. Lily of the valley was good not only for a stuffed nose but for loss of memory. Scarlet pimpernel could help remove an awkward splinter or prevent hydrophobia after a mad dog's bite. St John's Wort was prized not only for wounds but for bed sores and bed wetting. And, like rue and dill, a sprig of it hanging over the door kept you safe from harmful spells when witches were around.

Some of those old remedies are still in use, like wolf's bane as a heart sedative and chamomile for jangled nerves. But many others have long since gone out of favour.

It was into this old world of herbal remedies that Sir Robert Sibbald was born, with an urge to find which were the genuine remedies. For most of his life he had lived abroad and when he returned to Edinburgh in 1670 he immediately began to build up a private collection of plants on ground now occupied by St Anne's maltings. Five years later a better site was found for his growing collection in what eventually was known as the Old Physic Garden, adjoining the grounds of Trinity Hospital. Much of the garden's success was due to Sir Robert's young assistant, James Sutherland, who later became the University's first professor of botany. Rare plants were sent to

him from many parts of the world, including one from Abyssinia that was a potent cure for dysentery.

By 1689 there were 2700 different plants in the collection, all of them gathered with one prime purpose, to discover "what *materia medica* in the way of herbs Scotland was capable of producing". This knowledge was very soon put to practical use. Classes for chemists' assistants were run by Mr Sutherland, starting at the sensible hour of four or five A.M., to prevent the lads being late for work in their masters' shops.

In 1695 the Town Council recorded that the Physic Garden was "in great reputation both in England and foreign nations". With the passing years its value in the field of medical research declined, but in other respects its reputation has never ceased to grow. Out of it sprang Edinburgh's Royal Botanic Gardens, one of the most famous in the world.

It must, of course, be admitted that not all the seeds of medical research flowered as delightfully as the Royal Botanic Gardens. Corpses were needed for the surgeons, and relatives tended to be annoyed when the corpse of a loved one was snatched away overnight from the newly dug grave. In Greyfriars Churchyard the iron railings and massive slabs can still be seen, that were used in the early nineteenth century to foil those dreaded Resurrectionists. But the trade began long before that, in the days when heads and arms and legs of aristocrats still adorned the Tolbooth. As early as 1725 it was well established. The town was seething with rumours then that the young Professor of Anatomy was getting his corpses from local graves. There were angry scenes and the mob very nearly managed to storm into Surgeon's Hall. The authorities, scarcely less outraged, fixed heavy penalties for any who were guilty of this *crimen violati sepulchri*. But it still carried on.

We have to go back even further, however, if we want to meet the first of Edinburgh's body-snatchers. In 1582 the famous Scottish historian George Buchanan was buried in Greyfriars Churchyard. Soon afterwards a 24-year-old student persuaded the sexton to go into the churchyard one dark night and dig up the skull for him. The sexton was well rewarded, and the head-hunting student seems to have been no less content with his bargain, for he kept the skull all his life. Eventually he became the highly respected principal of Edinburgh University and on his death he bequeathed his treasure to the University with all the necessary evidence that this was the priceless skull of George Buchanan.

The University too seems to have been delighted with the generous gift. As early as 1689, visitors were being regaled with all the details and by the end of the century these had been recorded for posterity in a catalogue drawn up by the University librarian.

It was not only in medicine that changes were being seen in the late seventeenth century. The sedan chair was fast coming into favour and ladies of quality were no longer content to walk. Yet, even for them, Edinburgh was now a problem city. Many of the fashionable high flats were approached along closes so narrow that you couldn't get out of an ordinary chair on reaching your own house door. A new style of sedan chair had to be designed specially for Edinburgh — one with a door at the side instead of the front. And if you lived in a really steep close, then you got one with a swivel seat as well, to avoid the very real risk of toppling out.

Not only the ladies used sedan chairs. Old men and invalids used them too, on occasion, and into one of these categories fell Sir John Foulis of Ravelston. He frequented the baths that the Company of Surgeons provided for the treatment of diseases. They were not inexpensive. The use of the cold bath cost £3 10s sterling per annum, £2 for six months and 4s for a single bath. There were no season tickets for the hot bath, which cost 10s if you bathed alone and 5s if you had no

*There are times when even Old Man Death feels an overwhelming urge to lay aside his scythe and rest his weary bones amid the scenes of his triumphs in Greyfriars Churchyard.*

*Dean Village, about 1693.*

objection to company. Sir John did things in style and he had to pay extra for that. His account book shows that one visit cost him £3 "for sweiting in the balnes", 14s for canary, 14s for coffee and brandy, 14s 6d in tips to the attendants and £1 to the hackney chairmen who carried him there and back.

Edinburgh's special sedan chair was a blessing for those who used it. But much more than that was needed, to meet the challenge of the times. New ideas in architecture were needed as well. Though the area of the city was just the same as it had been a century before, the population had grown from scarcely eight thousand to fully twice that number, with prospects of a still further and even more rapid growth. The houses were becoming taller, the congestion only too apparent, and sanitation was fast breaking down. So a new kind of high tenement was devised, not with narrow closes for access but with a spacious square in front. That was much more wholesome.

The first of those squares was the so-called Parliament Close, which had been there since Parliament House was built in the 1630s. Bounded on the north by the Kirk of St Giles and the Luckenbooths, it had Parliament House on its west side and partly on the south, while on the east was the piazza, where many a business deal began. Though it was never really residential, latterly it had Bailie Robertson's tower of Babel on its eastern side.

Another half-century passed before the first residential square arrived, on the site of some old properties behind the Lawnmarket. Designed by Robert Mylne, the King's architect, it started a fashion which led eventually to the creation of the New Town. Much of Mylne's Square can

still be seen, with the date 1689 above the arched pend leading in from the street.

There was a need for squares like that. Though the Royal Mile was still being described by travellers as the finest street they had ever seen, vast quantities of lavender and rose petals were now required, to perfume the houses in the narrow closes. In Mylne's Square the fresh air came billowing up. Very soon James's Court was built beside it and other squares quickly followed.

It was not only in the heart of the city that new buildings were being erected. Down in the valley of the Water of Leith the stone masons were busy too, erecting more granaries to cope with Edinburgh's ever-growing demand. The Dean Village, all through the centuries, had been largely a village of millers where the sound of the water wheels echoed from dawn to dusk. By 1585 it already had eleven mills but these were not enough. Early in the seventeenth century the city erected a new one, six storeys high, on Millers' Row beside the river. Even that was too little. In 1659 the bakers of Edinburgh erected two kilns with a housing scheme for work people and in 1675 they followed it up with their "great house", the granary which still dominates the village. On the doorway of one of its projecting staircases, the frieze is inscribed —

GOD BLESS THE BAXTERS OF EDIN BRUGH UHO BULT THIS HOUS 1675

and in a panel above are emblems of their craft — two bakers' peels with a pie on one and three cakes on the other. "God's Providence is our Inheritance" says another inscription dated 1677. To this day the building is still very much as Slezer sketched it about 1693.

[131]

*"Here," wrote Slezer, "is one of the highest houses in the world, mounting seven stories above the Parliament Court and being built above a great descent of the hill, . . . so that from the bottom to the top one staircase ascends fourteen stories high."*

There were growing signs in the late seventeenth century that Edinburgh was losing some of its old medieval character, though much of it still remained. The merchants still started their business deals in the piazza and adjourned to some nearby tavern for the final stages. The taverns were a boon for the craftsmen too. James Howell discovered that, when he arrived from England with his boots worn out and ordered a new pair. Much to his surprise, the shoemaker gathered up a handful of tools and returned to the tavern with him. Turning a corner of it into a workshop, he made him a new pair on the spot. Even more surprising, the landlord came over with a chopin of wine and, settling down beside the cobbler, plunged into a lengthy religious argument that lasted until the boots and the wine were finished.

Howell perhaps was lucky. If they had not been so engrossed in religion, they would have been giving him a lesson on the King's English. Next to ungodliness the Scots abhorred slovenly speech. "They are great critics in pronunciation," wrote Thomas Morer in 1689, "and often upbraid us for not giving every word its due sound." It seemed so silly that the English pronounced "enough" as if it were written "enow" or "enuff". They neglected the "gh" as if it had not been written!

But not even the Scots' affection for a well pronounced word quite matched their flair for pageantry. As organisers of pageants they had a reputation as international as it was in the reign of James IV. A great nobleman's funeral, with lords in attendance and professional mourners, colourful hatchments and all the rich solemnity of death, was a memorable sight. For the heir it was as costly as death duties.

There was, for example, the Duke of Rothes. A General in the Scottish army, he became one of the highest State officials, latterly holding the office of Lord High Chamberlain. Seldom has such an unforgettable funeral passed along Edinburgh's Royal Mile.

In tribute to his martial deeds two regiments brought out their artillery and led the long procession in mourning posture. Then came the two conductors, and the Little Gumpheon or Mort-head, the first of the many banners. The professional mourners followed close behind — fifty-one Poormen, all soberly dressed in gowns and hoods, and carrying armorial banners.

A mounted trumpeter and a fully armed cavalier on a fiery steed heralded the second array of banners — the Pencil of Honour, the coats of the noble houses of Abernethy and Leslie, and the Standard of Honour — followed by the dead Duke's warhorse with two of his lackeys in attendance.

Then came two trumpeters on foot, marking the next stage in the procession. The Bute and Carrick pursuivants introduced a still more impressive group of banners, the Great Gumpheon, the Coat of Abernethy in mourning, and the Little Mourning Standard. Fourteen of the Duke's friends followed, two and two, and then came the Kintyre and Dingwall pursuivants, and the Duke's spurs and gauntlets, his corselet, targe, helmet and dagger, each held high by a gentleman. His favourite saddle horse was led by two of his lackeys in livery.

Edinburgh's public bodies were well represented. First came the civic fathers — the old Council and the new, twelve of each, with the four bailies, the sword-bearer, the mace-bearer and the Lord Provost himself walking alone. The city's clergy followed and the masters of the Town s College, including the Principal. There were more gentlemen and barons, Writers to the Signet and advocates, the town clerk and the clerk of the Court of Session, the Commissaries of Edinburgh, the macers of the Session, and the Lords of Session with their Lord President.

By then the procession was approaching its climax. An attendant held in his arms the robe that the Duke had worn as Lord High Chamberlain. The Officers of State came into view — the Registrar, the Lord Justice Clerk, the Lord Treasurer

Regiments with the
Artillery & Equipage marched
all before the Proceeding in
a Mourning Posture.

Conductors.

the little Gumpheon.

Poormen in

A Cavalier armed at all points

The Colours of y Defunct.

Servants of y Defunct in

The Horse of Warr led by
two Lacqueys of the Defunct.

Close Trumpets.

Two Pursevants

Bulle Carrie

*Funeral of the Duke of Rothes*

and Hobos in Number fifty one.                                        T. An Trumpet.

The Pincil of Honour.    The coat of Abernethy    The coat of Leslie    The Standard of Honour.

reat Gumphed    The coat of Abernethy    The little Mourning Standard    Fourteen gentlemen of the Defunct's friends
Mort head.       in Mourning

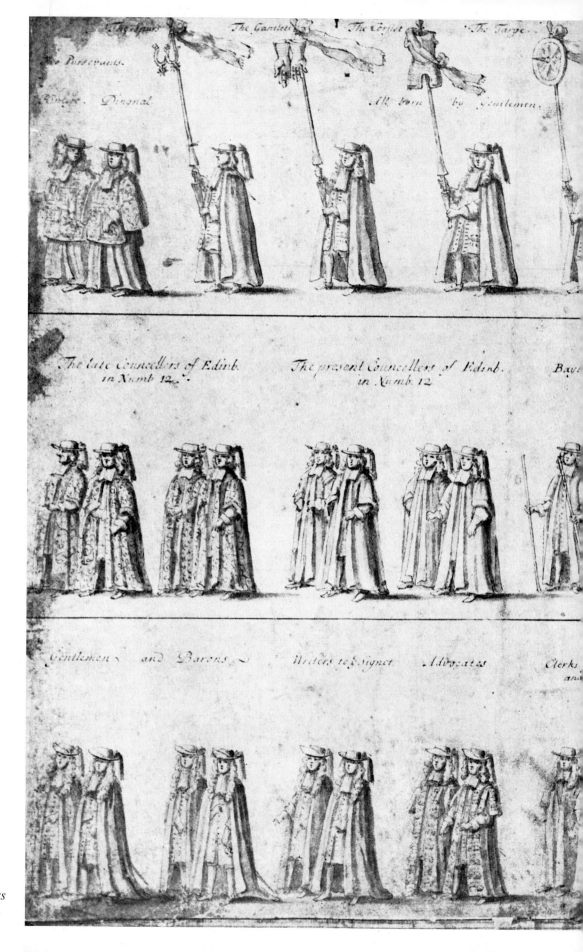

Funeral
of the
Duke of Rothes

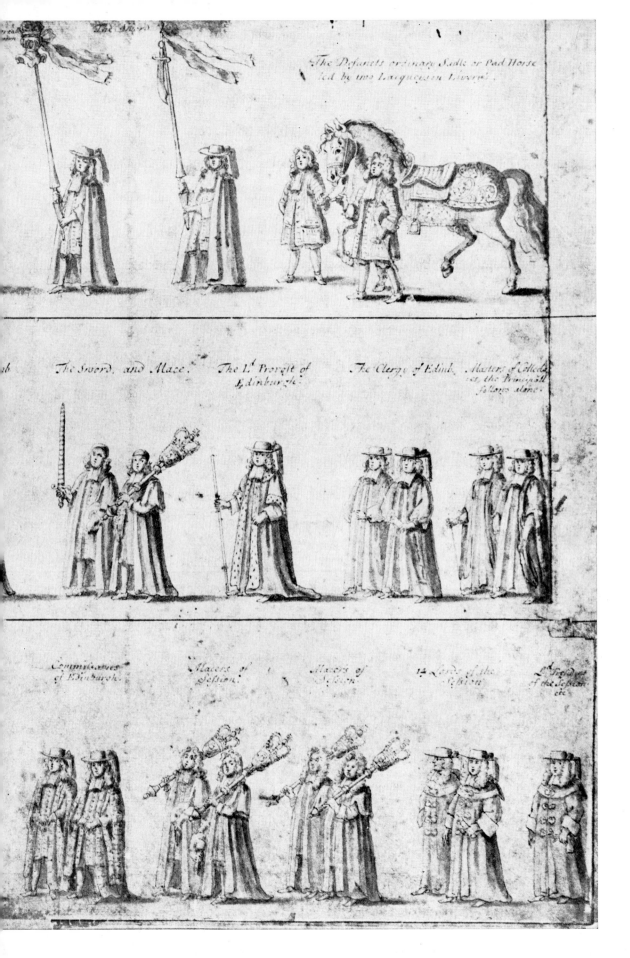

The Defunets ordinary Sadle or Pad Horse
led by two Lacqueyes in Liverys.

The Sword, and Mace.    The L.d Provest of    The Clergy of Edinb.    Masters of Colledg
                        Edinburgh.                                    -es, the Principall
                                                                      follows alone.

Commissaires    Macers of    Macers of    14 Lords of the    L.d President
of Edinburgh.   Session.     Session.     Session.           of the Session
                                                             etc.

*Funeral
of the
Duke of Rothes*

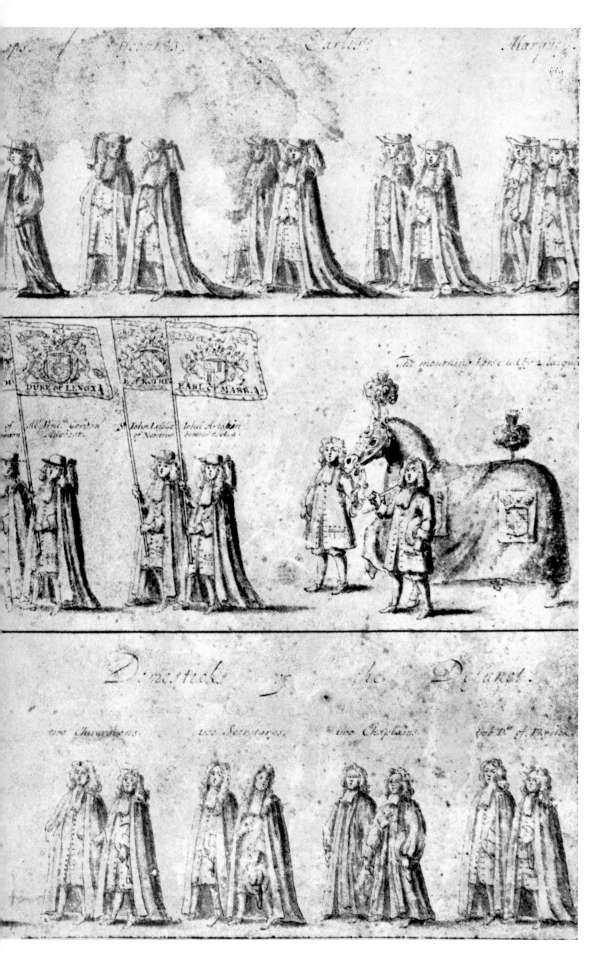

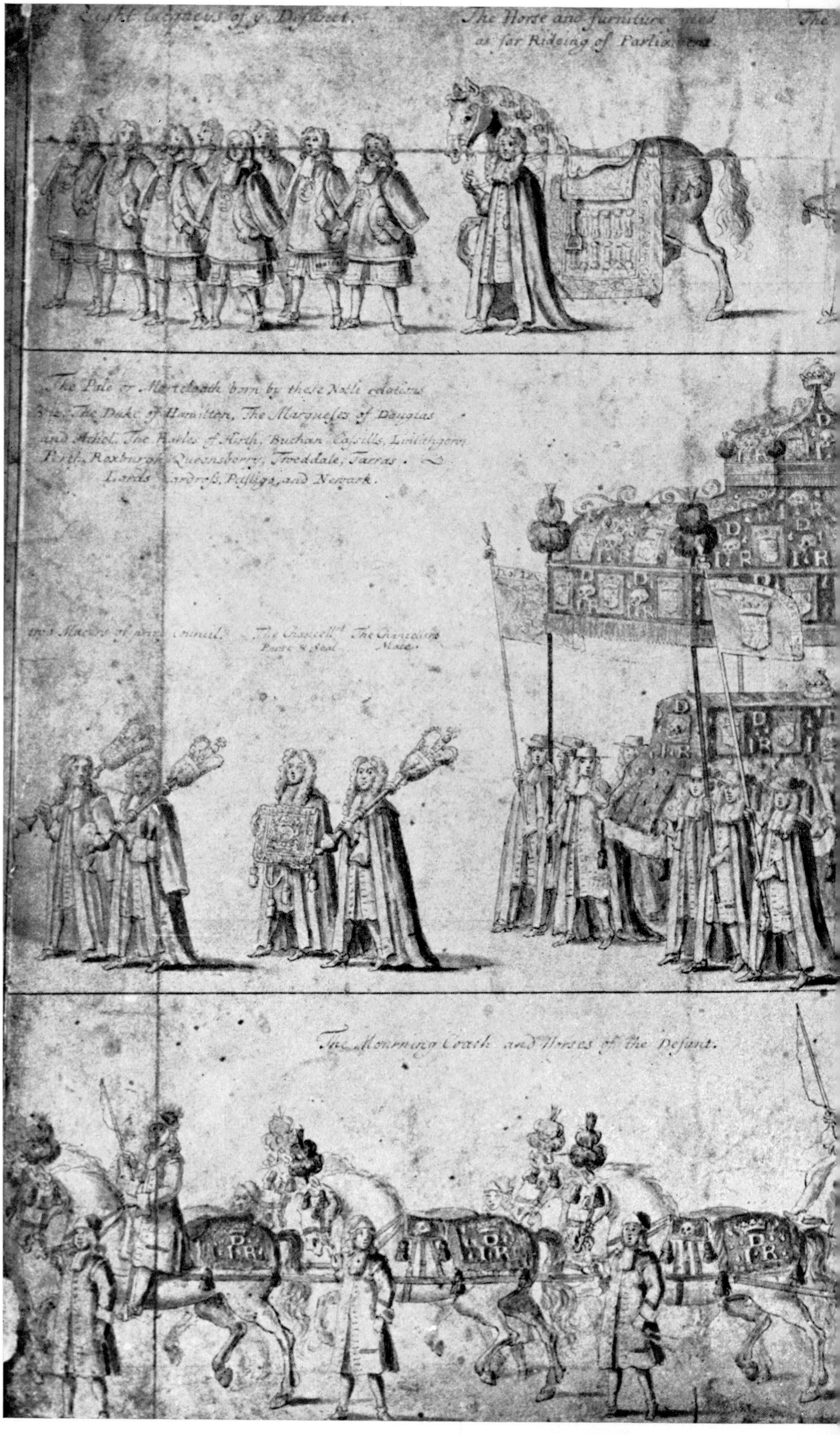


*Funeral of the Duke of Rothes*

Bishops.  Lyon King of Arms.  [Chancellor] Bishop.

Sr Robt Sinclare Bt  Sr Charles Areskin Bt  Sr Tho. Moncrief of this Bush  The [...] Thesaurer

The Canopy, or Pale Supported by Noblemens Sons Viz.
Ld Murray, Ld Charles Hamilton, Lords Lorn Bargh Livingstoun,
Glamis, Crightoun, Ogilbie, Yester, Boyd, Cochran, Inverury with Maisters
Ld James Murray, Maisters of Kingston, Forbes, Ross, Balmerino, Burleigh,
Melvill & Prestage. Besides severall Barons Knights & Gentlemen who
attended near ye Body to assist ye Relicts the Noblemen in thier turns.

The Chief Mourners in Gowns and Hoods in number [...]

Marq. of Montros ye Earle              tenn Lords Assistant to the Chief
Dow: of Laures of Hadington,                        Mourners.
ye Pannel.

Two Trumpets and Kettledrum followed by his Maties
Troop of Guards which closed ye Solemnity.

and Lord Advocate, then Barons, Bishops, Sheriffs, Earls and Marquesses.

Two more pursuivants, Unicorn and Ormonde, and two more trumpeters heralded yet another stage — a parade of the colourful standards of Earls and Dukes, each borne by a gentleman. John Erskine carried the standard of his brother, the Earl of Mar. Alexander Haldane of Gleneagles was standard-bearer to the Earl of Tullibardine. Then came the Duke's mourning horse with its ornate saddlecloth and its sombre plumes, and the Master of Newark carrying the Great Mourning Banner.

Trumpets sounded again and there were the six heralds this time — Islay, Albany, Marchmont, Rothesay, Snadown and Ross. They were followed by the Duke's domestics — his surgeons, secretaries, chaplains and doctors of physic, two of each. Then eight more lackeys preceded another of the Duke's horses, wearing the magnificent saddlecloth that had only been seen at the Ridings of Parliament.

The ducal coronet was borne along, on a tasselled cushion. Behind it came the Archbishops and the Lyon King of Arms with two baronets in attendance, followed by the macers of the Privy Council. The Chancellor's Purse, his Seal and his Mace came next, just in front of the ornate coffin with its magnificent mort-cloak and matching canopy. A Duke, two Marquesses, nine Earls and three Lords carried the mort-cloak. More than twenty noblemen's sons bore the canopy.

Walking behind the coffin were the chief mourners, among them the Dowager Marchioness of Montrose and the Countess of Haddington in gowns and hoods, with lords in attendance. Behind them was the mourning coach with its six horses. And then came the last of the trumpeters and a drummer on horseback leading the King's Troop of Guards in a final eye-catching display.

It was a funeral long remembered by the Duke's family. The Government, they had understood, would be meeting all the expenses. Too late they discovered their error. The cost had been almost £3000

sterling and a hundred and twenty years later some of the bills were not yet settled.

But even more memorable than death were the Ridings of Parliament, the most magnificent of all the processions that graced the Royal Mile.

It was only on rare occasions that people saw this grandest of Scottish spectacles. There was one in 1669, when James Brome was among those who watched with delight all the flower of the Scottish nobility.

"And indeed," he wrote, "it was a very glorious sight, for they were all richly accoutred and as nobly attended with a splendid retinue. The heralds of arms and other officers that went before were wonderfully gay and finely habited, and the servants that attended were clad in the richest liveries. Their coaches drawn with six horses, as they went rattling along, did dazzle our eyes with the splendour of their furniture, and all the nobles appeared in the greatest pomp and gallantry.

"The regalia, which are the sword of state, the sceptre and the crown, were carried by three of the ancientest of the nobility, and on each side the honours were three mace-bearers bare-headed, a nobleman bare-headed with a purse, and in it the Lord High Commissioner's commission. Then, last of all, the Lord High Commissioner with the dukes and marquesses on his right and left hand. . . The officers of state, not being noblemen, ride in their gowns. All the members ride covered, except those that carry the honours, and the highest degree and the most honourable of that degree ride last."

On those occasions the cavalcade itself was not the only spectacle. For days, before and after, the Royal Mile was alive with gilded coaches and lackeys in livery and ladies in robes of rich brocade. All the cream of the Scottish nobility was there and many a nobleman from across the Border and overseas as well.

Another of those great processions was held in 1685. We know more about it than any of the others, for sketches were made at the time and two of these have

*Arthur's Seat from the Queen's Drive*

The
Riding of
Parliament

4

The Gentleman Usher with his white Rod.

to y.e High Commissioners Commission.

...ter of y.e Horse.

The Duke of Hamilton.

Two Trumpets.

a Kettle drum.

The Captain at the head of his Ma.ts Troop of Guards, 10 Trumpets & Kettledrum.

*Queensberry House*

survived among the treasures of the National Library of Scotland. One is reproduced on pp. 144-5, showing the Marquis of Douglas carrying the Crown of Scotland, with the 1st Duke of Queensberry, the King's Commissioner, a short distance behind, and then another Duke and two Marquesses, in this procession of the Three Estates up the Royal Mile. In 1976 it could serve as a foretaste of less colourful scenes to come.

Fifteen years later the last of those great processions was held in 1700, when the 2nd Duke of Queensberry was the King's Commissioner. Eight miles from the city he was met by the magistrates and a retinue of nearly forty coaches and 1200 horse accompanied him to Holyrood-house.

The whole scene was graphically described by Hugo Arnot, the Edinburgh historian. Horse Guards and Foot Guards lined the Canongate, with the city's trained bands from the Netherbow to Parliament Close. At the door of the House, waiting to be first to greet the Commissioner, the Lord High Constable sat in an elbow chair with his personal guards on either side. But there nearly wasn't a State Opening that year, for Parliament House only narrowly escaped destruction a few months earlier, in the most disastrous fire the Old Town has ever seen. People say it originated in the home of Lord Corserig, one of the Lords of Session, and certainly at an early stage this one-legged judge was seen "naked, with a child under his oxter, hopping for his life."

It was among the lawyers' houses around the Meal Market that he lived. But the fierce wind quickly swept the flames uphill from the Cowgate through the Kirk-heugh to Parliament Close and the soaring tenements at its eastern end. These went up like tinder.

All through the night there was panic. The water cisterns were empty but no one anyway was interested in fighting the flames. They were far too busy dragging their household goods into the street to augment the confusion. It had taken eleven years to build the highest of those tenements and in eleven hours they were heaps of rubble.

Maybe the townspeople had some excuse for abandoning the fight at the start. The heat was unbearable and even more terrifying were the showers of sparks, whirling everywhere in the gale-force wind. Those sparks, said one eye-witness, were "like showers of snow, they were so thick. It was to me an emblem of Hell and oftentimes Sodom came to my mind that night."

There was, in fact, a widespread feeling that this was no ordinary disaster — that God was making Edinburgh suffer for its sins. Even the Town Council recorded in its minutes that the great growth of immoralities in and around the city had brought this fearful rebuke from God.

But whether or not it was an act of God, there was no denying the damage. Duncan Forbes of Culloden had seen the Great Fire of London as well as this one, and it was the Edinburgh fire that he found the more terrifying.

"All the pride of Edinburgh is sunk," he wrote to his brother. "From the Cowgate to the High Street all is burnt and hardly one stone is left upon another. . . . These Babels, of ten and fourteen storeys high, are down to the ground and their fall is very terrible."

It was one of the most fashionable parts of Edinburgh which vanished that night. The Lord High Commissioner had lodgings there. So had the President of Parliament, the President of the Court of Session and most of the Lords of Session. Two hundred families were left homeless. But it might have been very much worse. All through the night the sparks showered down on Parliament House and the Kirk of St Giles, but still by a miracle they escaped and no lives were lost.

Though Parliament House had been the meeting place of the Three Estates since 1639, even without that fire its days were now numbered. Plans were going ahead for a Union of the Parliaments of England and Scotland. The details, it is said, were worked out at an informal meeting in the gazebo at the foot of the

Moray House garden. In March 1707 the "Honours of Scotland" were brought down from the castle for the last time, to grace a meeting of the Scots Parliament. After that they were returned to their chest in the Crown Chamber, the little window was sealed with masonry and for over a century they remained unseen.

But that year's most memorable day was undoubtedly May Day. In the morning the bells of St Giles rang out a merry carillon: "Why should I be sad on my wedding day?" And an exciting wedding day it was for everyone. The presbyterian Whigs were delighted, for it marked the consummation of all their efforts to achieve a happy Union with England. The less happy Jacobites were there as well, to jeer in ineffectual protest.

Oddly enough, if we can believe an old tradition, the one person with most cause to be sad on that wedding day was the grand architect of the Union, the 2nd Duke of Queensberry.

The Duke's town house can still be seen, close to Holyroodhouse, at the foot of the Canongate. Since then it has been heightened and spoiled by the addition of an extra storey and the removal of the original ogee roofs, but it is still a handsome building.

People tended to weave legends round the Queensberry family. It was very well known that when the 1st Duke died he was carried off to Hell by the Devil in a coach and six. The 2nd Duke was heading that way too. His eldest son, the Marquis of Drumlanrig, was an idiot.

That May Day, all Edinburgh flocked to watch. Even the attendant of the mad young Lord Drumlanrig joined the rest, leaving him locked in his room. The hours slipped past. Flushed with success the Lord High Commissioner returned home to find that in his absence his son had broken loose and roamed the house. Down in the kitchen he found its only occupant, a young servant boy, turning the meat on the spit. So he took over the kitchen boy's work, with the boy on the spit instead of the roast. He was already eating the half-roasted body when the kitchen staff returned.

It was not only in Queensberry House, however, that the Act of Union roused unhappy memories. Many a wealthy Scotsman made his home in England after that, and Edinburgh felt a sudden blight which left it withered for half-a-century. A very different city emerged after those fifty years but that is another story.

# APPENDIX

# The Old Illustrations

EARLIEST OF the old illustrations of Edinburgh is a sketch measuring $10\frac{1}{2}''$ x $17\frac{1}{2}''$, in the British Library (Cotton MS., Augustus I ii 56). Giving a bird's-eye view of the city from the north, it shows troops on the outskirts and many of the house roofs badly damaged. The Cross of St George is recognisable on the banners of a column approaching Holyroodhouse through the Water Port and there is little doubt that the sketch records the sacking of the city by the Earl of Hertford in 1544.

Enlargements of two details are reproduced here. On page 67 Holyrood Abbey and Holyroodhouse — "the kyng of Skotts palas" — are shown with Arthur's Seat and Salisbury Crags in the background. The city itself is on p. 68, with several recognisable buildings — the Netherbow Port, St Giles', the Church of St Mary-in-the-Field and the Black Friars monastery.

There was another English raid in 1560, to drive the French garrison out of Leith, and this produced a second picture map, now in the Petworth House Archives of Lord Egremont. It shows Leith in the foreground, under siege from four warships as well as land forces, and Edinburgh in the background. Four details from this map have been included — the castle (p. 24), Leith (p. 73), Holyroodhouse and Arthur's Seat (p. 74) and the town of Edinburgh (p. 77).

In 1647, at the request of the Town Council, James Gordon of Rothiemay drew a bird's-eye view of the city. Measuring $16\frac{1}{4}''$ x 41", it was engraved in Holland. From it the Royal Mile is reproduced (pp. 103-7), the Church of the Holy Trinity (p. 32), James Mosman's house (p. 62), the Magdalen Chapel (p. 66) and Moray House (p. 109). The Flesh Stocks can be seen at the top of the Canongate on p. 105. They were removed when the Canongate fleshmarket was opened in 1673. So, when Andrew Johnston made the first British engraving of Gordon's map about 1710, he omitted the Flesh Stocks and inserted five water wells which had been erected along the Royal Mile in 1674. The list of streets, closes and important buildings was also omitted from this later version.

Where the map is numbered, details have normally been given in the text. On p. 32, however, they are not included and there the key is —

p The College Kirk   t Trinity Hospital
57 Hackerston's Wynd   u St Paul's Work
58 Leith Wynd   i Leith Wynd Port

The illustration of Holyroodhouse on p. 114 is also believed to be by James Gordon of Rothiemay.

The most beautiful of the old picture maps of Edinburgh, by the Bohemian Wenceslas Hollar, is in the Royal Library at Windsor Castle. Though it is dated 1670, it has been argued that the map itself must be about twenty years earlier, for the Tron Church is shown without its steeple and Heriot's Hospital is still unfinished. It might be equally well argued, however, that the correct date must be 1670, because the windows were certainly not there in 1650.

Until now the only copies of this engraving were taken from a very early photo-zincograph, made for inclusion in Part III of the National Manuscripts of Scotland 1895, and much of the fine detail of the original was lost in those reproductions.

The original has now been re-photographed. The whole engraving, which measures $15\frac{1}{2}''$ x $24\frac{1}{2}''$, is shown on p. 151 and there are enlarged details in the frontispiece and on pp. 108, 119 and 120. The key to the map is: —

| | |
|---|---|
| 1 The Castle | 14 The Outer Court of |
| 2 The Weigh House | the Palace |
| 3 St Giles Church & | 15 Trinity College |
| Steeple | Church & Hospital |
| 4 Parliament House | 16 Grey Friars Church |
| & Courts of | 17 Heriot's Hospital |
| Justice | 18 St Magdalene |
| 5 The Tron Church | Chapel |
| 6 The Netherboll (sic) | 19 Bristo Port |
| Gate | 20 Potterrow Port |
| 7 The Cannon Gate | 21 St Mary Port |
| 8 The University | 22 West Port |
| 9 The Minthouse | 23 St Cuthbert's |
| 10 The Abbey of | Church |
| Holyroodhouse | 24 The City of Leith |
| now the Palace | 25 The Firth of |
| 11 The Abbey Church | Edinburgh |
| 12 The Gatehouse | 26 Inchkeith Castle |
| 13 The King's Gardens | 27 The Free School |

The Dutchman John Slezer provided another set of memorable engravings of Edinburgh. Settling in Scotland in 1669, he married a daughter of the Laird of Lauriston, in Kincardineshire, and became a captain of artillery. About 1678 he began his mammoth task — the recording "of all the King's Castles, Pallaces, towns, and other notable places in the kingdom belonging to private subjects".

In 1693 he published the first edition of this *Theatrum Scotiae*, in which the first two plates were of Edinburgh. One of these showed the Dean Village in the foreground, with Edinburgh and the North Loch beyond. Details from this engraving are on p. 29 and pp. 130-1. Parliament House and the high tenements, on p. 132, are from the other plate.

In an article in the "Bannatyne Club Miscellany", vol. ii, Captain Slezer is also given the credit for a unique set of six drawings on Royal paper, that are now among the treasures of the National Library of Scotland. Four are of the funeral in 1681 of the Duke of Rothes, Lord High Chancellor of Scotland. The other two show the start and finish in 1685 of the "Riding of the Scots Parliament", the spectacular cavalcade which preceded the first session of any Parliament in Scotland. There is little doubt, however, that the artist was in fact Mr Chalmers, the Herald Painter to James VII. The drawings came into the possession of a Mr Howard, in England, and on his death they were sold at Covent Garden in 1766 by public auction. The buyer was Thomas Sommers, an Edinburgh glazier, who soon afterwards had engravings etched from them. There is a set of prints from the engravings in the Edinburgh Room in the city's Central Public Library.

The original drawings came to the National Library through the Advocates' Library. Sommers sold them to the Faculty of Advocates in 1803, for preservation in their library, as "memorials of two of the most splendid exhibitions of Scottish national pomp and parade extant". Five of the six originals have now been photographed for the first time and are reproduced on pp. 134-41 and 144-5.

The pages from Bishop Elphinstone's Breviary were photographed in the National Library of Scotland.

The following are the sources of the other old prints:—The Giant Stag of the Canongate (p. 17), from J. C. Innes "Liber Cartarum Sancte Crucis" (Bannatyne Club), p. 301; Dirleton Castle (p. 20) and St Margaret's Well (p. 40), from R. W. Billings "Baronial & Ecclesiastical Antiquities of Scotland" (1909) vol. ii. facing pp. 125 and 198; Couci Castle (p. 21), from MacGibbon & Ross "Castellated & Domestic Architecture of Scotland" (1892), i. 37; Church of the Holy Trinity (p. 37) and the Netherbow Port (p. 99), from W. Maitland "History of Edinburgh" (1753), facing pp. 140 and 207; St Triduana's Well (p. 39), from "Transactions of the Scottish Ecclesiological Society" (1911), iii. 239; Holyrood about 1647 (p. 114), from "Bannatyne Club Miscellany" i. facing p. 188.

ERRATUM

P. 102, ll. 21-2 — For "Captain John Slezer"
read "Gordon of Rothiemay".

[150]

*"The Citie of Edenburgh" by Wenceslas Hollar*

# Index

*(Illustrations are in italic numerals)*